THE OVERNIGHT CEO

THE OVERNIGHT CEO

A Story of Adversity, Grit, and
Turning Lemons into Lemonade

LADEIRA POONIAN

Published by GFB™, Seattle
www.girlfridayproductions.com

Produced by Girl Friday Productions

Cover design: Emily Weigel
Production editorial: Kylee Hayes

Image credits: cover © shutterstock/Franck Legros; shutterstock/nopparada samrhubsuk

ISBN (paperback): 978-1-967510-13-9
ISBN (ebook): 978-1-967510-12-2

Library of Congress Control Number 2025911959

First edition

To Aaliya and Samara, In the obstacle course of life, may you appreciate the challenge of the climb, relish in the thrill of the moment and always find time to enjoy some ice cream.

CHAPTER 1

I've spent the past two decades trying not to remember the details of that night.

And now, as I attempt to tell its story, some things still grip me with the same intensity they did then. Others seem to have fallen out of reach for good.

I'd made a quick weeknight dinner—was it chicken? Likely, with potatoes and vegetables. After dinner, our son, Naveen, had gone to his room to study and, eventually, to sleep. I heard my husband, Amrik, check on Naveen before heading to his office to read. Amrik's mother had passed away nearly a year before and, following Sikh tradition, there was to be a memorial gathering on the first anniversary of her death. Before that gathering could take place, it was Amrik's duty to read slowly through the entirety of the sacred scripture—a process he'd been engaged in every evening for months.

"You know, I've still only read two hundred pages," he'd said, just before heading upstairs. "But I have been dreaming of my mother so much these past few weeks."

"She probably wants you to hurry up and finish that book so she can have her anniversary service."

I cleaned up from dinner, vacuumed the rugs, and eventually settled into bed around 11:30 p.m. I remember looking over at the clock when Amrik climbed in beside me: 12:07.

It couldn't have been more than an hour later when Amrik gave a jolt. In the ambient light, I could see that his head was lifted up off the pillow, his eyes wide open, nearly bulging out of their sockets. He was screaming like a frightened child.

"Amrik, wake up!" Had he dreamed of his mother again? "Amrik, Amrik! *Wake up!*"

His head dropped back, his body newly languid.

"Mom! What's wrong?" Naveen was already there at our bedside, breathless.

"Help me get him to the floor, Naveen, then call 911."

My god, Amrik was a deadweight. It surprised me that Naveen and I didn't drop him.

I heard Naveen's panicked voice on the phone with emergency services as I counted compressions. At just the moment when I opened my mouth to breathe into Amrik's, he took in a gasp of air, then quietly, gently let it out as my face closed in over his. His exhale mingled with my own deep inhalation.

I knew he was gone.

The paramedics were running up our stairwell within minutes. One of them escorted me and Naveen downstairs and positioned us in the front hallway. I called our good friends Anjali and Jatin and asked them to come by the house and pick up Naveen.

Then Naveen and I just stood there, looking over at one another, unsure of what to say or do.

"We'll get through this," I offered.

We could hear the defibrillator in action: the high-pitched revving, the clack of its discharge. The dull steadiness of the straight line that followed each attempt.

The paramedics rushed Amrik down the stairs, past us, and started loading him into the ambulance.

Before I knew it, I was sitting next to the ambulance driver, and we were already pulling away from the house. I turned back to see Naveen still standing in the driveway as Anjali and Jatin pulled in. Thank god they had arrived in time to sweep Naveen into their car and take him away from the house.

Later, all heroic actions attempted and ceased, the hospital staff offered me time with Amrik at his bedside. I stroked his hair and thought about the celebrations we'd been planning for the year ahead: Amrik would turn fifty in February, we'd celebrate our twenty-fifth wedding anniversary in the summertime, and Naveen was going to turn sixteen in the fall.

"This will be a year to remember!" we'd bragged to one another just days before.

There was a shuffling of feet in the hallway outside Amrik's room. I turned and met Naveen's gaze through my tears. Anjali and Jatin were there with him. I could see in Naveen's face the recognition that his father was now gone forever.

The four of us stayed with Amrik for some time, crying, hugging, struggling to make sense of what had happened. There hadn't been time to think in the hours and minutes leading up to this moment, and now here we were, at the cusp of having to contemplate what the world would be like without him. Anjali was chatting with Amrik as if he might still lob some sarcasm in her direction—the two of them were close, like siblings.

Both Naveen and I stayed with Anjali and Jatin that night. The next morning, the two of them made calls to notify people of Amrik's death. It was as if, without my saying so, they knew I had no desire to talk to anyone.

We were shocked when Naveen insisted on going to school, saying that he didn't want to sit around all day thinking about what had happened. Not a handful of hours later, he was back with us. His schoolmates and teachers had also been surprised by his decision, and eventually Naveen himself realized that he needed the rest of the day, and the rest of the week, to regain his composure enough to pay attention in class.

Not more than a couple of weeks prior, Amrik had brought home a packet of documents for me to sign. Estate plans, trust documents—I'd signed wherever he'd pointed, and then we hadn't talked about it again. But the day after he died, there were already inquiries from the insurance company.

"Ma'am, I am obligated to ask: Did you have a hand in your husband's death?"

"How can you ask me something like that?"

"Ma'am, we have to turn every stone."

"You have no idea about our relationship."

"Yes, ma'am. But we have to ask. It's happened before. You'd be surprised how many women have done it."

That evening, Naveen and I returned home, and our good friends the Singhs—Jai and his mother, Sushma, both worked at Amrik's software company—brought food for the little group of people who were still helping to make calls, assist with paperwork, and plan Amrik's memorial.

It would be days before Amrik's true cause of death was revealed: arteriosclerosis. One of his arteries was 90 percent clogged, another 95 percent, and a third 75 percent. By then, family had started to arrive for the funeral—both of Amrik's brothers who lived stateside; my sister Zarine, who lived in England; and my brother Phillip, from Trinidad. Friends were still coming by offering food, support, and company. In all, there were about twenty people staying with us from the Wednesday after Amrik died through the weekend after his funeral. They'd all just come in and taken over areas of the house, and I was relieved they'd seen to making themselves comfortable. Some were staying in bedrooms, others were sleeping on couches, and Naveen's friends were coming by in the evenings to visit with him. The house was bustling with activity, much of which I participated in, very little of which I remember.

The week passed in a blur, including the funeral services, Amrik's cremation, and the departure of everyone except Phillip and Zarine, who had made plans to stay with me and Naveen for several weeks.

Frankly, what most stands out in my memory of those days is this: Not even twenty-four hours after Amrik had died, Jai started teaching me how to use a computer.

My husband ran a software company, so we'd had computers in our house for decades, but I'd never even turned one on.

When it came to knowing about Amrik's business, I knew enough to tell people that his software helped simplify and streamline complex manufacturing processes, and that was that. Amrik took care of the business and all our finances, and I took care of Naveen, the house, and the garden, and continued to work a few days a week as a high-risk obstetric nurse.

Jai showed the patience of an elephant. I couldn't focus; I couldn't think. But he sat with me for hours every night that week to ensure that I understood the basics. Computer on, computer off. Open an email, reply, add an attachment. Generate a new email. I was sorry that Jai felt obligated to teach me, but I appreciated his determination to ensure that I'd be able to communicate with Amrik's employees. It was clear that Jai had already pictured something I hadn't: I was going to have to make my presence known at the company's office as the inheritor of Amrik's business.

At one point, Jai said as much outright: "Ladeira, you can't go into the office and not be able to respond to an email. There are basic things you have to know *before you go in.*"

I couldn't make sense of his quiet faith in me, the respect he showed me even though he was witnessing firsthand the depth of my ineptitude. Jai didn't want me looking like a fool, and he took it upon himself to make sure that I was at least minimally capable and ready.

By Sunday evening, the house had transformed into a different space once again. The grandfather clock ticked louder than before. The heavy scent of already-decaying floral arrangements followed us from room to room.

"Naveen, come sit with me and talk." It was the first time we'd been alone together since we'd stood over Amrik's body before the paramedics arrived.

"I don't want to talk about it, Mom." He shocked me with his assertiveness. "Let's just focus on the good things."

CHAPTER 2

The red lines on the alarm clock came slowly into focus: 8:53 a.m. It was late, but I had no intention of getting out of bed.

Thoughts drifted in and out, sometimes racing past, sometimes lingering until my gut tightened and another wave of nausea would push my eyes closed.

Here is my whole life, shattered right in front of me . . . Sixteen is such a critical age, and Naveen and Amrik were so close—the two of them always plotting against me and giggling at their great success . . . My god, that boy could go either way— he could end up being so angry, so bitter . . . What if he falls in with the wrong group? What if he gets into drugs? How am I going to help him? . . . What about all those people who depend on Amrik for their livelihoods? What do I say to them?

When I'd asked him years before if there was a place for me in the company, Amrik said he'd have his HR department look into it and then never spoke about it again. I knew the last thing he wanted was for us to work together. Back when he was building his own company, he'd rented and shared office space with husband-and-wife business partners who fought, out loud and in front of everyone, nearly every day. They were a laughingstock among their employees. Amrik bristled at the thought of becoming like them.

"I need you to know there are people in the company that I just don't trust, Ladeira." Amrik had said this to me just weeks before he died, on one of our evening walks around the neighborhood.

I'd pried a bit: "Tell me why."

"Bill's taking luxury business trips with his girlfriend—do they think I don't know they're having an affair? Then, just the other day, Bill got into it with Nina, berating her—swearing at her!—in the middle of their presentation to potential clients. I know I made him vice president because I could see him as my right-hand man, but I don't like this whole other side of him."

I'd squeezed Amrik's hand to let him know I understood his distress.

"Ladeira," he repeated, this time with greater emphasis, "I need you to know there are people at work who just can't be trusted."

I rarely had contact with Bill except to chitchat with him and his wife at company gatherings. At the time, I hadn't pried. I felt for Amrik, without question, but I personally didn't need to keep track of who was trustworthy and who wasn't.

Why had he said it that way—that he needed *me to know?*

"Mom?"

Naveen had entered the room without my noticing.

"Mom. You've got to get out of bed. Your job now is to be at the office."

My job?

These people don't know me from squat. I might be a high-risk OB nurse, but to them I'm just the owner's wife. These are highly trained people in their own right, well experienced in the software industry. How is a person with no clue going to lead them? They need someone with knowledge, with vision, not someone who just learned to send an email.

"Naveen, let's go downstairs and I'll make you some breakfast before school."

"Mom, you have to get dressed and go to the office." Naveen was firm. His tone surprised me. "I'm going to school, and you have to go to work."

How quickly he'd stepped into the role of man of the house.

"Naveen, I can't get up. I can't deal with this right now."

"Dad used to go on business trips a lot. Let's look at it like he's on business, traveling for a while, and we are both just waiting for him to come back." He paused. "And while we wait, your job is to go to the office."

He turned to leave, and as he did, I slung my feet over the edge of the bed and leaned my body forward.

What am I going to say to them when I get there?

I moved toward the shower.

Just two days earlier, Naveen had asked me, "Are we going to have to move out of this house?" We had just moved in a year earlier. I knew that we had Amrik's insurance money to fall back on, but to Naveen it must have looked like all the changes we'd recently made—including the big upgrade from our house in Mission Viejo to a seven-thousand-square-foot custom home in Coto de Caza—were newly threatened by Amrik's passing.

I'd answered him, "No. We are fine. We don't have to move from the house," and assumed that would be enough to make him feel better. I was only thinking about how we'd continue to have shelter and food, but Naveen must have been wondering whether he'd be able to continue at his private high school, stay on the tennis team, keep all his new friends.

I stood in front of my closet.

Nursing uniforms. Clothes for going out. Nothing suitable for *my new job*. In less than two weeks' time, Naveen's friend Ricky's mother, Sally, would intervene by scheduling a fitting for me with a Nordstrom stylist. She'd given that stylist a list of items I needed, and I purchased nearly everything Sally recommended. Pants, jackets, blouses, accessories—all of them office appropriate, all of them good quality, some I'm still wearing today. But on that first morning, I had to conduct a careful search.

I settled on a pair of black pants and one of my plainer shirts.

Amrik had given his life for his work, and I wanted us to be able to take pride in his legacy. Naveen was right that I needed to show everyone at the office I wasn't turning my back on them.

Naveen isn't going to let me feel sorry for myself, for us. Things like this happen in life, and what we need to do is take one day at a time. Deal with whatever comes up. I can do that. We can do that.

I found my keys and walked out to the car.

If I mess this up, at least I can say that I went to the office and tried to take care of Amrik's people. I owe that to Amrik and to Naveen.

I didn't want to go to the office, but if there was something that scared me even more, it was the thought of Naveen, grown, with disappointment long settled into his face: "You didn't even give it a go, Mom. Why didn't you even try?"

CHAPTER 3

It was coming up on lunchtime when I pulled into Amrik's reserved parking space. I took the turn a little wide; thankfully no one was parked in the adjacent spots. *Good enough,* I thought.

The last time I'd come by the office was to meet up with Amrik for a lunch date. I'd brought some vegetables from our garden—mostly okra and peppers at that point in the season—to leave in the break room for whoever wanted them.

Visiting the office was usually quite a lot of fun for me. I'd drop by with either the latest crop of vegetables, fresh flowers to decorate employees' desktops, or a pot of soup or some other treat I'd cooked, and then I'd make my way to various employees' desks for a little chitchat. I was well aware that Amrik wanted there to be a strong sense of community at work—for everyone to feel part of a close-knit family. So, when I visited, I made sure to make the rounds.

It didn't hurt that I liked finding out what everyone was up to, though I would describe myself more as a busy bee than a busybody. I sensed that most people liked my visits and appreciated the attention they received from the boss's wife.

The boss's wife.

Many times, I'd stood by Amrik's side at company gatherings, smiling, amiable. But most of the time, he socialized with the team on his own. Once each month, he arranged a catered, company-wide event; employees from all the different departments would gather for drinks and a late-afternoon meal. And almost weekly, Amrik would linger after work with some of his closest confidants, either imbibing at the office or heading over to a neighborhood bar. On some of those evenings, Amrik would call to let me know I wouldn't need to worry about feeding him dinner when he arrived home.

It made good sense to me that Amrik wanted to form a work community that felt like family. After all, the company had gotten its start among friends in our family home in Mission Viejo not more than a handful of years ago. He and his brilliant friend Frederick (who would later become the company's chief technology officer) would sit in the living room and talk from six in the evening until dawn the next morning. They'd banter and argue about everything in the wide world from politics to physics to the details of their work projects. Eventually, they'd come to imagine and invent the technology product—ShopFloor 2000—on which Amrik would build his software business.

Frederick was a true friend to Amrik, a good man, and a welcome guest in our household. The refrain "Frederick is coming over" was so expected that whenever it was uttered I knew to prepare not just for a dinner guest but also for an overnight guest. I'd set up a comfortable space for Frederick to retire should he and Amrik decide to pause their conversation before morning.

Frederick was like family. He appreciated whatever I offered for dinner and adored every curry I made. Indian food, Trinidadian food . . . Frederick was perfectly unfussy, but that man could make a mess! He never drank alcohol, but if you were to walk into the room where he'd spent the night, you would think he'd been living in there for a week, not just nodding off for a couple of hours. The man could splash water around a bathroom sink and mirror like nobody's business!

Frederick and Amrik had a similar energy about them. And like Frederick, Amrik was never satisfied and easily grew bored with work, always wanting more from his jobs—sometimes more than they could offer. Eventually, Amrik started his own consulting company: Telecom Solutions, Inc. That was when our house truly became an extension of his workspace. Some of the time he worked in his upstairs office, and some of the time he worked in Naveen's playroom—a multipurpose room just to the right of our home's front entrance. Amrik converted the playroom closet into a mini computer center, and occasionally his friend and accountant Angel would come by, set up a square card table, and fill it with all the company papers, receipts, and her printing calculator. I'd come into the room to see Naveen sitting on the couch, watching a children's show, with Angel seated at her table just behind him, the rhythmic *zhe zhe zhe* of her calculations accompanying the television voices. In the evenings, Amrik would read Naveen a bedtime story, then I'd hear him ask gently, "May I leave you now?" adding, "Dada has to go back to work."

The shift from telecommunications consulting to software design and production had been the product of friendships, conversations, good timing, and good luck.

I suppose it all started when I'd taken Naveen to a department store to pick out a birthday gift for one of his friends. He and I were standing at the register when a woman waiting behind us tapped me on the shoulder.

"Are you from the West Indies? My husband is from Trinidad, and you have his same accent."

Lola was from Jamaica, and she was also there to select a gift from the registry. She and I became fast friends and were exchanging telephone numbers before we left the parking lot. Lola's husband, Felix, and Amrik ended up getting along marvelously, and the four of us grew to be close.

Felix worked in procurement at McDonnell Douglas—the aerospace manufacturing company that would later become Boeing. The men were always talking shop, and in one of their conversations Felix hit on the idea to develop a product that would solve a major production hurdle. The professionals at McDonnell Douglas were wasting *hours* consulting giant manuals whenever they needed to learn how to proceed with mission-critical processes. Felix identified the operational pain point and then Amrik, in all those long evening conversations in our sitting room with Frederick, envisioned and built a platform that would provide easy access to process manuals and flow all the production processes through multiple computers or workstations at once. That way, everyone involved with a project could have immediate access to relevant information and real-time process updates. That was in 1994. Amrik's software—and I can say this with certainty now that it's become the dominant software platform in manufacturing environments—was a product ahead of its time. A couple of decades ahead, to be more precise. Even its name, ShopFloor 2000, was a nod to innovations that would characterize the coming millennium.

Felix got Amrik an audience with McDonnell Douglas leadership, and Amrik convinced them to invest $1 million in proof of concept. Acknowledging the information he'd received from Felix about his company's prior attempts to overcome this particular manufacturing hurdle, Amrik included a line in his sales pitch that sealed the deal: "You've already spent $99 million this year on options that haven't proved viable or useful. Why don't you use that last million to give my product a try?"

That all-important meeting had taken place just five years

ago. Now here I was, seven days after Amrik's death, sitting in the car outside his office, wondering how I would be able to preserve the company he'd dedicated himself to building.

This time, I entered the office building with just my purse in hand.

"Good morning." I greeted Sharon at the front desk, and her eyes and mouth opened wide. I maintained a steady pace toward the staircase. The sooner I got upstairs to Amrik's office, the better.

I wasn't in his space for more than a minute before people began to come by and welcome me. They were all very pleasant, and I was glad to see them, but I also felt called on to perform. A confident woman, not a scared one, was who they needed to see. Otherwise, they might start jumping ship, and Naveen and I would be left with a company that had no employees—a company that would be forced to fold.

Confident woman.

I'd played that role a thousand times before, but always in relation to other people's fear and grief, never my own. A career in high-stakes nursing had taught me how to put up a front, how to work with patients whose lives we were trying to save. How many times had I told a dying patient, "Everything is okay," when it wasn't, hoping to enlist their participation in life-sustaining procedures? The same strategy felt necessary here. I needed everyone to see me and believe "Ladeira is a strong person. Everything is okay."

Surely they're all out there wondering what will happen with their jobs.

I sat at Amrik's desk and turned on the computer—my first big achievement since entering the building.

The prior week's intensive training with Jai would get me through the rest of the afternoon. There were hundreds of emails awaiting a reply. I felt thankful that many of them were about nothing more than scheduling upcoming meetings.

Everyone here is a brilliant engineer! What on earth could I possibly contribute besides agreeing to these meeting requests?

Carefully, I typed, "Yes. I can attend at that time. Thank you," then located and hit the Send button.

The people in these rooms and at those desks are people who loved Amrik. They believed in his vision and the value of the software. Many of them helped produce it!

I noticed a couple of employees walking down the hallway outside Amrik's office. They nodded and smiled; I returned their nods in slow motion.

It's okay. Everything is okay.

On that last visit I'd made to pick up Amrik for lunch, he hadn't been in his office when I arrived. I'd seated myself in his black leather chair and leaned back, stretching my legs out in front of me, checking my cell phone while I waited. Sharon, who played roles as diverse as front desk assistant and benefits administrator in this start-up environment, had paused in the doorway when she saw me. "Ladeira!" Her smile was always cheerful.

"Meet your new boss!" I'd teased her.

The memory of that playful joke churned my stomach. I shifted uncomfortably in Amrik's chair.

"Ladeira is *here*?" I heard Bill's voice in the hallway and straightened my back a bit. Time for another show.

"Ladeira. What are you doing here?" The question sounded accusatory. Bill stepped into the office before he added, "You should be at home taking care of Naveen."

"I'm fine, Bill."

"No, no. You should be at home. Why don't you stay home with Naveen, and let me take care of the company for you." He wasn't asking a question so much as giving a directive.

"I'm fine, Bill. Thank you for your concern."

"All right, then, Ladeira." He turned on his heel and walked off.

Here was the one person that Amrik made sure to tell me he could not trust telling me to go home so that he could run the company. I hadn't come to the office knowing exactly what I was going to do, and I had an even more limited sense of what I *could* do that would be at all helpful. But the one thing I knew for certain was that I intended to find a way to honor Amrik's life and legacy. And I was starting to see what that would entail—I would have to be present, learn everything I could as quickly as I could, and make sure to keep an eye on Bill and any others like him who might view Amrik's absence as an opportunity to put themselves in charge.

Within days, I checked in with my supervisor at the hospital. "Ladeira," she assured me, "so long as you keep your license active, there will be a job here for you. For now, I'm going to hold your position open for six months before we try to fill it. You let us know what happens there, and you just tell me when you're ready to return."

I was lucky to have such a supportive team of nurses at work, and incredibly lucky to have a familiar job to return to should I need. But there was no way I could keep the house and keep Naveen in private school on my nurse's salary. For now, it was enough to have the assurance that I had a career to return to, and that Naveen and I absolutely could *survive* on that salary if we needed to.

Software company CEO.

The title seemed laughable, but for now, I was going to have to make it fit.

I finished responding to emails, then decided I should step out of Amrik's office and visit with some of the staff. What else was there for me to do with myself except talk with people? And besides, I wanted them to know that I was here, that they were not going to be abandoned, that I would do what I could to preserve the business and their jobs. That afternoon, I sat down one by one with those I knew I could trust and conveyed my determination to take care of their needs as best I could.

I stayed late that day—and many more to come—trying to gather my thoughts about how to proceed. Before heading to the car, I made a list of things I imagined I could begin taking care of right away:

1. Employee well-being and morale.
2. Providing the tools that people need to be successful in their jobs.
3. Improving productivity and efficiency.

That would be enough to get me started.

CHAPTER 4

I was the eighth of nine children—five girls and four boys. My eldest sister was fifteen years my senior, and my little sister was younger than me by four years. Growing up, it felt like we were two families; my older siblings were married and starting families of their own when the four of us younger ones— two brothers, three and two years older than me, me, and my younger sister, Zarine—were still children. All nine of us were close in the sense that family members were constantly in and out of each other's homes, dropping by to check in or share a meal, and spending time together on weekend outings to the beach. Besides the three siblings closest in age to me, I spent the most time—sometimes whole summers—with my eldest sister, Sarina, and her family. Her first child, Yvonne, was about nine years younger than me, and I could help with her care.

When she wasn't gardening as a pastime, my mother was consumed with her businesses. She had a contract with a nearby government-owned coconut plantation and employed local workers to cut and dry the coconut meat for sale to the coconut factory in Trinidad's capital city, Port of Spain. She and my father would make regular trips to Port of Spain, sell the dried meat to be made into oil, then treat themselves to a big dinner of Chinese food. There were always leftovers, which my brothers, my sister, and I would devour just as soon as they came through the door.

Besides managing her business drying coconuts, my mother had purchased and rented out several homes in the area. She also owned a pub on our town's main street. That was her primary business. Like most people who had homes on the main drag, we lived in the upstairs flat and utilized the downstairs as a moneymaking investment. Our downstairs neighbors included markets, bookstores, and other pubs, and then there was a cinema, a McDonald's, and a supermarket filling out the street. As with other families' kids, each of us children worked downstairs at some point—my siblings and I were usually behind the bar taking payments, serving up bottles of alcohol, and calling out the finger-food orders when they were ready for pickup. We'd come home from school in the afternoons, do homework, maybe work a bit in the kitchen, then work the bar when the pub got busy—around seven or so in the evening until about nine—before our mother would take over. Everyone coming from work at the Texaco refinery would pass by the front of the pub, so there was an active scene there from the end of the workday until around eleven or midnight. Later in her life, my mother would turn over running the pub to my brother Phillip so she could partner with another savvy businesswoman in town selling snack foods to the workers as they passed by in the daytime on their way to and from the refinery or in the evenings after having enjoyed themselves at the pubs along the main street.

To tell you the truth, we kids were my mother's employees. When my siblings and I weren't working in the pub, we were helping her in the garden. My mother had carved out a space on the coconut plantation to grow okra, peppers, eggplant, and tomatoes. There was a stream nearby, and as little kids, we would go back and forth between stream and garden to water the plants. From watching and helping my mother, I learned about mixing mulch and fertilizer, prepping soil, seeding the soil properly, and ensuring that the vegetables got the right amount of water to thrive. I still grow those same vegetables in my own garden today, and I'm well aware that my love of gardening comes from enjoying that time with my mother and my closest siblings.

My father worked the bar at the Royal Hotel in San Fernando, just a few miles from our house, serving tourists from all over the world and listening to their stories. He would work at night, then come home and sleep through the mornings, wake up, talk with my mother at the kitchen table while eating a quick meal, then head back to work in the evening. He was loving and affectionate, and he spoiled me and my younger sister, Zarine. He would bring us treats—mangoes, papayas, guavas, and other fruits from the hotel's many trees; ensure that we were his first dance partners whenever there was a house party; and collect S&H Green Stamps so that we could fill the stamp booklets and redeem them for our choice of special chocolates. Though I saw him a lot less, I felt closer to him than to my mother, perhaps because she was a businesswoman who didn't have the time or the inclination to spoil us like he did. When it came time for dinner or for sleep, it was the women from among the workers at the coconut plantation who would make sure that we ate and were tucked into our beds for the night. I remember my father's hugs, but I have no memory of being hugged by my mother. I understood that she loved us dearly, but she didn't show it in the ways I might have wanted or needed.

Even when it came to money, my mother showed the boys more love than the girls, for example, paying for weddings. If any of my brothers had wanted to go to university, my parents would have supported them. But none of them aspired to do that. They were drawn to becoming trade professionals, self-sufficient in their own ways. One of my brothers is a mechanic; he can take an engine from any car, take it apart, and put it back together just like that. He's always telling me, "You know, I do all this work, and sometimes people don't have any money to pay me." I suppose he takes enough pleasure in the activity itself that if he gets paid, great, and if not, that's also okay. I've always told him that he should move to America and start his own business. He could make a lot of money here with all the knowledge that he has.

From an early age, I would listen in on my parents' kitchen table conversations. My mother would talk about the people who hadn't yet paid their open tabs at the pub and how she was going to humiliate them into giving her what they owed. My father would talk about the different people he met at the hotel: "So, this man's daughter is studying to be a lawyer, and the son is a surgeon," or "Can you believe this man is building a fortune selling electronic devices!" Maybe he said it explicitly or maybe I read it in his facial expressions, but I internalized what I took to be my father's primary wish: that one of his own children would have a professional career that he'd be proud to talk about with his customers.

My older siblings had all done well for themselves. They were married with steady jobs, many even growing families of their own. One of them worked at the Texaco refinery, another became a priest. Every one of them was living a life one might thoroughly expect of any Trinidadian. If you're from the island, you don't leave. You work at a restaurant, a jewelry shop, the Texaco plant. You make a living and enjoy island life: You go fishing, you entertain your family, you go to the beach.

Not me.

I didn't like working in the pub, and I didn't want my life to resemble those of my siblings, first helping out in the pub, then getting married shortly after graduating high school—or even before graduating, like my brother Elijah had done at the tender age of sixteen—then focusing on raising a family. That life trajectory was even more the expectation for us girls: From a young age, we understood that we were supposed to help out around the house and with the business, then get married and keep our own homes. I also understood that my mother was tight with her money and would not support my continuing my education once I turned eighteen. I wanted to be able to support myself and not depend on my parents, and I wanted to make my father proud by being the successful professional he could brag about.

To help set a path in the direction I wanted, I took advantage of opportunities offered through school. The government regularly recruited students from my high school to do secretarial work, so I secured one of those jobs to begin the summer after I graduated. I made many mistakes using a manual typewriter. No one ever fired me, but on the one occasion when I managed to turn out a document with few errors, my supervisor did draw undue attention to it: "You know, Ladeira, why can't you do something like this all the time?" When I mentioned that I was thinking of applying to nursing school, he was enthusiastic: "You *should* go to nursing school, because you are not cut out for this!" I took that as just the encouragement I needed to find work more suitable to my temperament and ability.

Nursing met my need for independence and for a professional education that interested me. Best of all, as a student, I would be required to work in the hospital when I was not in class, and I would be paid enough for that work to support myself. I applied and started earning my nursing degree in Trinidad, but quickly felt I was missing out on something. A number of girls were leaving to get their degrees in England, then coming back to the island, where their foreign credentials earned them a certain amount of prestige and the possibility of moving quickly through the ranks to become department heads. I wanted that for myself too.

So I applied to study in England, where one of my older sisters, Hana, had already moved.

Hana had gone on vacation to visit a cousin there, met her pen pal correspondent, and promptly married him. Her new husband, Robin, was a good enough writer. My sister Zarine and I used to read with great attention the letters that he sent to Hana, appreciating and occasionally giggling at his story-telling imagination and his extravagant language. From the letters, we could see why she had developed an interest in him; he seemed like a smashing guy.

My parents had been furious with Hana for coming home from vacation married to a man she'd essentially just met. There was drama. But as I understood it, my parents' distress was far less about the fact that Hana had eloped and far more focused on the fact that she'd married a man they believed was absolutely wrong for her. When we met him, I was stunned by how overwhelming, how insistent, was the discrepancy be-tween his letters to Hana and his actual person. I don't think it's at all unfair to describe him as a loser or a deadbeat.

They say that opposites attract, but even in my youth I could see the drawbacks to this adage; attracting your oppo-site is not always a good thing or a sign of true compatibility. Robin and Hana were like night and day. Hana was an absolute light, an extremely outgoing person, and beautiful—she was crowned Carnival Queen! In Trinidad, she was the personal assistant to one of the British managers who oversaw the sugar plantation. She had a good job. She had great connections. And she had a bevy of Trinidadian men lining up to date and marry her—guys with great professions, high status, and good looks, that is, guys who would have given her a very good life. By contrast, Robin was twelve years older than Hana. He was ambitionless, worked baggage control at an airport, and lived with his parents.

Hana spent a few months at home, then quit her job and moved to England for good. Though her leaving had been stressful and the family had fussed, she'd opened a door for me. With my sister already living there, I felt I could make a reasonable case for moving to England, and to Exeter, where Hana and Robin lived, to complete my degree. I applied, and the university interviewed Hana in my stead. Of course, that they met and vetted her stood in my favor. I was invited to join the program there.

As expected, my mother was resistant to the idea. She didn't like parting with money, so she made clear to me that she had no intention of paying for my transport. Of course, she was also not keen on losing yet another helper in the pub.

My father, on the other hand, was delighted. "You," he said to me one afternoon, "*you* can do anything you set your mind to doing." It was my father who, in no uncertain terms, instructed my mother to purchase my plane ticket to England. Before I left, he spoke to me words that would influence every decision I made during my time in England and for the rest of my life: "*Beti*"—he used the Hindi word for "daughter" to let me know how serious he was—"I have protected you and taken care of you up until now. Now, you have all the rope in the world. Do not hang yourself with it."

I didn't realize how much leaving family and friends and everyone I knew as a twenty-year-old would shake up my sense of self. Everything about moving to England was exciting, until the moment I realized, *Oh my god! I don't know anyone here except Hana!* Initially, I didn't get the impression that the English were the warmest of people. And besides that general impression, I quickly became aware that the housekeeping staff at our nurses' residence were convinced that I'd accidentally made my way to their school from a totally uncivilized world. To convey their distrust, they'd regularly check my locker to see if I'd stolen anyone else's belongings.

One day, one of them asked me outright, "How did *you* get to England?"

"Oh, I climbed a high tree and then jumped vine to vine until I arrived right here," I teased.

From the looks on their faces, I could see that they believed me.

They may have come from the countryside to keep house at the nursing school in Exeter, but I was from a third-world country. For them, England was de facto more cultured, more sophisticated places than Trinidad.

During my first months at school, I'd tacitly agreed with them. In the West Indies, we had all believed that everyone in England was very sophisticated. Trinidad had long been a British colony, and growing up, we all felt inferior to our British counterparts in-country. To this day, I believe that if I hadn't had my O-Level exam qualifications, I wouldn't have gotten into school at Exeter. I understood that because I was from Trinidad, something more was required of me; I was held to a higher standard and had to work doubly hard to prove myself.

I'd come to England because I, too, believed that white people were better and more privileged, and that if I got my degree from a predominantly white country, I would earn a better standing on my own. I don't think I had a complex about it, but for quite some time I did assume that the students—no, the people—in England were more advanced, and better equipped, than me.

At first, it blew my mind that there were uneducated people in England and that a lot of them didn't know anything at all about the high standards I was held to in the West Indies. I can say for certain that if I hadn't lived there myself and met a lot of people, I never would have believed that some of them weren't very intelligent. It was a discovery that saddened me. I learned from questions like "Do you have running water and electricity where you're from?" that the people around me might be more prejudiced than they were smart. I remember talking to a patient who asked me where I was from, and when I answered, "Trinidad," he said to me in response, "Oh yeah, I've been to that part of Africa." Experiences like that taught me that there are a lot of people in the world pretending to know. But then they open their mouths, reveal their ignorance, and don't even recognize that ignorance enough to account for it, let alone apologize for it.

I decided early that there was no point correcting them and that my false belief in my own inferiority in relation to the British was my own fault, a lack of awareness or education on my part about the way the world really is.

Still, it surprised me when I realized that I was more prepared than most of my classmates. I learned, for example, that our patients were able to understand my speech better than that of their other attendants. When I started classes, I'd tended to think that my fellow students must be sharper than me and prepared myself to accept the fact that I might come out at the bottom of the lot after our exams. But when the first set of results came in, I'd placed third. Later on, when it came time for us to take our board exams for license to practice as registered nurses, I excelled. It wasn't until that late point that I remember thinking, *You know what? I am smart!*

It was not the case that people in "advanced" countries were necessarily more advanced than me. Where I came from hadn't inhibited my potential for success. I'd taken advantage of the educational opportunities offered me, and they were good. Back when I first transferred my school credits from Trinidad to England, hadn't I learned that I had achieved the same as the O-Level exam takers? And hadn't some of the girls starting nursing school at the same time not even completed a high school education?

Thankfully, unlike the housekeeping staff, my fellow students were very nice and respectful of one another. We were all in the same boat. All of us were away from home, so I guess that is how we all became friends. We would all go together to the pubs around town. It's true that we formed smaller friendship groups among ourselves, but we were all good to each other. Frankly, the only time I sensed that there was any competition among us—and perhaps it wasn't competition so much as desperation—was when someone would leave leftovers or a prepacked meal in the communal fridge. Then, it was every woman for herself.

CHAPTER 5

I was thankful to have Phillip and Zarine stay at the house with me and Naveen during those early weeks following Amrik's death. Zarine had visited us many times before. Her husband worked in Saudi Arabia for several months at a time, and she would take vacation from her job as a pediatric nurse and visit for a month, sometimes a whole summer. Phillip and Zarine were self-sufficient; they were in and out, helping in the kitchen, just talking and spending time with us. Phillip had discovered and then so quickly fallen in love with our jacuzzi that Naveen, Zarine, and I spent most of our time trying to coax him out of it so that he wouldn't overheat. He would stay in there for six hours at a time, thoroughly enjoying the contrast between the cool December air and the heated water and plotting out how to build a jacuzzi for himself once he returned home to Trinidad.

When Zarine and I were little girls, Phillip—who was nearly a decade older than us—would take us to the fair and buy us tickets so that we could go around playing all the games. He'd give us specific instructions—"Now be sure you go here, and there, and then over to that one"—so that we wouldn't miss any of the best games or the ones offering good prizes. He also liked that he could spend time chatting with his girlfriend while Zarine and I were busy trying to see what we could win.

After he left California to return to his wife and the family pub, and to start building his own jacuzzi, Phillip would return to visit us just once, for a bowel resection surgery. I knew all the best doctors and surgeons in the area, so I brought him to stay with us to ensure that he got excellent care. Phillip didn't have health insurance, but I negotiated a rate for him and paid cash for the procedure. The surgery was a success, and though we didn't see each other frequently after he healed, we stayed in close touch. Every now and again, Phillip would go out drinking with his friends, get a little tipsy, then a little sentimental, and call me up to say, "Ladeira. You know this home in Trinidad will always belong to our family." By that time, Phillip was running the pub and living in the family house. "So long as I am here, this will always be your home." I appreciated him saying that more than he knew. Our mother had skimped and saved to buy and keep that property, and she herself had always talked about it as a kind of refuge. She always said it was a place where her children could come if things were not right with their lives.

In his seventieth year, Phillip was shot dead in the pub. Over a period of time leading up to his murder, the town had grown more corrupt, more lawless, and the pub had been robbed on a regular basis. Also on a regular basis, the local mafia had come by to offer Phillip protection—for a fee. Each time they offered, Phillip refused. He got so used to being robbed that he would anticipate its happening and just hand over the money. But on the night he was murdered, there was no robbery. The gunmen had knocked Phillip's wife, Dolores, unconscious and taken his life, but they hadn't otherwise touched or stolen a single thing from the pub.

We never discussed it, but I don't think Phillip ever

thought he was under any greater threat than simply being robbed on the regular. However, after learning that he'd been killed, I sensed that Phillip had been made into an example for other business owners: If they failed to secure the mafia's protective services, this would be their fate.

Zarine and I both were scared to return to Trinidad for Phillip's funeral. There was already a systematic practice of targeting Trinidadians who lived outside the country and returned to visit family. Our clothes, our speech, our movements distinguished us no matter how we might have tried to blend in. I found it difficult to tell Dolores of my decision not to attend his funeral: "I don't know what the killers' motives are, and I'm afraid to come there—let alone to bring Naveen with me." She was disappointed but didn't press the matter.

I dealt with my shock and sadness by going to the nursery, buying too many plants, and working in the garden. After Amrik's death, I'd learned to close my mind to certain thoughts and feelings and to focus, instead, on more practical matters.

I still think fondly of those days that Phillip, Zarine, Naveen, and I spent together after Amrik died. Even Phillip's near-dangerous appreciation of the jacuzzi had been a welcome distraction, and it was good to have family show such genuine enjoyment of our home and its amenities. When we'd moved to Coto de Caza from Mission Viejo, Amrik had insisted that we build a custom-designed house. That meant our living arrangements underwent a significant upgrade in a relatively short period of time. The Mission Viejo house—in which we'd lived for a decade—was a reasonably sized tract home. We could easily call to one another from across the rooms, and there was even a little space along the side of the house for me to have a garden. But the Coto house was big—over seven thousand square feet—and fancy, with marble pillars, wood inlaid ceilings, ornate moldings, multiple fireplaces, and in the yard, a big area for me to garden and a tennis court and pool for Naveen.

When we made the move from Mission Viejo to Coto, I didn't tell any of my nursing colleagues. Eventually one of them noticed that I was arriving to work by a different route than usual. Only then did I admit that we'd purchased a new home. Everyone was excited that we'd moved to Coto and wanted to come over to see the house. But that possibility felt awkward to me. We nurses didn't usually socialize outside of work. Honestly, we barely socialized *at* work, given how intense and fast-paced our jobs were. We were lucky to spend a few minutes together in the break room here and there, and in those moments we were likely to find ourselves talking about the different cases we were working on or the status of a critical patient, rather than our personal lives. A lot of the nurses would come to me, describe something that had occurred, and ask, "Ladeira, what should I do?" I was like a consultant to the group of us. It was true that in that group, I'd never heard any nurse speak ill of another nurse. Still, I didn't want to show off the house to them, much as they may have been excited for our family's move.

I was even more nervous about the reactions of some of the people in the friend groups Amrik and I socialized with. Financial status was very important to many of them, and several were constantly vying to prove that they were better off than the rest. Instead of being happy when friends acquired nice things—a new car or home—there were some who'd raise their eyebrows and say things like "Lucky him, eh?" or "Look at that new car. I wonder what they did to get that!" I worried about being looked at differently, suspiciously, about being the subject of conjecture. And I didn't much appreciate the plain old nosy people either. I remember a couple of friends who went out of their way to visit every builder working on a new home in the area, asking, "Is *this* the Poonian house?" Once they finally found ours, they dropped by unannounced on an afternoon that we also happened to be visiting the property, just to ask us how it was coming along. "Who does things like that?" I'd wondered aloud to Amrik as we drove away.

Amrik and I were excited to have what we did, but neither of us ever wanted to show off. He may have wanted to have a home with details that people would notice and appreciate—like Phillip enjoying the amenities, Naveen and his friends hanging out in the pool, or a guest commenting on the wood inlay—but neither of us wanted to be the object of anyone's jealousy or resentment. Instead, Amrik had pictured our new home as a gathering place—for events from family holidays to employee picnics. We would barbecue and people could swim in the pool or play tennis or other games in the yard. In his vision of things, everyone enjoyed themselves fully.

During that first month after Amrik's death, I did something out of the ordinary for me. I invited everyone from the office to our house for an afternoon. I was looking for ways to reassure them that I cared about them as much as Amrik did and wanted to make them happy with their work. Ted, who had been one of Amrik's first hires and was head of Research and Development at the time, came into the yard and exclaimed, almost theatrically, "So *this* is the product of all our hard work!"

Ted's comment, and the resentment motivating it, hit hard—as I imagine he'd intended. My old worries about the resentments and jealousies among our friend group had found a new focus: the resentments bubbling up among Amrik's closest business associates and team members. In that moment, I decided never again to invite anyone from Amrik's company to the house. The next day, I mentioned my frustration to our across-the-street neighbor, a sweet man who owned his own business. He shared a similar story about inviting employees to his home. From inside the restroom, he overheard a little group out in the hallway. One of them commented, "So this is where our money goes!" and the others followed up in the affirmative with "mm-hmm" and "I know, right?"

If Ted's comment had been his only one, or even the first of its kind, I may eventually have changed my mind about entertaining at the house. But that wasn't the first time Ted had challenged me in the weeks since I'd come to own the company. When a group of us was in the break room at lunchtime, I'd noticed spilled coffee on the floor and immediately nabbed a towel to start cleaning it up. "Why are you doing that, Ladeira?" Ted admonished me. "You're the head of the company!" Thankfully, I'd had my wits about me and answered, "What makes me so different from other people, Ted? If I see something that needs to be taken care of, I'm going to take care of it."

Ted's dissatisfaction with me could be even more explicit. On one occasion, he berated me for not keeping up Amrik's tradition of going out with the men on Fridays after work. "*You* are no Amrik. And you will *never* be Amrik."

As if I'd ever imagined I could be!

"That's right, Ted. I am not Amrik. And I am not going out drinking with the lot of you on Friday afternoons."

Ted may have been among the more vocal, but he wasn't the only person walking around the office in those early days and weeks expressing some version of the thought "*I* should own this company, not her." I suppose I could count on Ted to say to my face—and for everyone to hear—what others may have been careful to say only in private. At least Ted gave me the opportunity to reply. When Ted actually said to me, "I should own this company, not you!" I offered a reasonable answer.

"Well, Ted, Amrik married me. As a result, I am the owner of this company."

I should have known before inviting everyone to the house that, with Ted and some of the others jockeying for position and noticing every move I made, I would need to be guarded at all times.

CHAPTER 6

The power plays at the office were becoming more and more obvious. I noticed that Bill was holding meetings without telling me about them, and once he had the nerve to interrupt one of the meetings that I had been invited to attend. When he noticed me there, he barged into the room, announced, "Ladeira, I need to speak with you," pulled me out into the hall, and then instructed me not to return to the meeting, saying, "You really don't need to be in meetings with the employees."

This man had called me out of a meeting to tell me that I should not be attending meetings.

I stood motionless and watched him walk all the way down the hall before reentering the room and resuming my place in the conversation.

The employees who showed great loyalty to Amrik, and who transferred that loyalty to me, would keep me informed about Bill's maneuverings. As it turned out, Bill wasn't just telling me not to engage in meetings; I heard he was also going around telling everyone else not to speak with me about their work. It seemed he didn't want me to know what was going on in the company.

I focused my day-to-day activity on doing the exact opposite. I needed to get oriented as quickly as I could, so I spent time talking to anyone willing to engage in conversation with me. During those early discussions, I was careful not to make employees aware of how little I knew. Instead of asking all the questions in my head outright, I would simply inquire, "What are you working on right now?" That would start people talking, and I could guide the conversation from there. "So tell me more about the customer in that situation. I'm sure they're worried about what's going on. What's been your feedback to them so far?"

At the first in-office gathering we held after Amrik's passing, I made sure to announce to the group that I was eager to hear from them. "I don't know much about software, but I depend on you to help me, to guide me. I *will* be asking questions. To me, those questions are not stupid. My background is in medicine, not software. Bear with me and understand that I want to learn." I added: "I want the legacy of my husband to continue on through this company's success. He gave his life for this company. I want to see his dream come true."

I sensed that many people realized I was present every day and motivated to learn, and that I genuinely wanted to make the business work. I wasn't going to sell the company, and I wasn't going to bring in a new CEO to run it—at least not until I understood everything I could. I also wasn't stupid. When someone explained something to me, I learned quickly and didn't need to ask a question twice.

All my talking and checking in on people's work ended up being mutually beneficial. Many felt they were being well coached by me and thanked me for my interest in their projects. From my twenty-eight years in nursing, I'd learned to be an attentive and accurate observer of others. My ability to help patients in need hinged on paying careful attention to them— their appearance, their mood, and their words as much as their vital signs. I used that same "hands-on" approach with everyone in the company. I attended every meeting I could, and I made myself available to employees so that they'd feel comfortable seeking me out when they needed help, or wanted to strategize, or simply had an idea to share. In meetings and in one-to-one conversations, I was planning with them, encouraging them, and helping them determine next steps.

Without necessarily being aware of it, they were helping me do the same, especially when it came to providing me with valuable information and filling in the gaps in my understanding of internal and external business processes. I gathered as much information as I could without arousing suspicion. My method was similar to what Naveen called crowdsourcing: I made my rounds and talked to everyone to find out where the story was the same and where there were discrepancies among people's accounts. Then I could follow up on those discrepancies until I got to the heart of what was happening. Those conversations were incredibly eye-opening for me, especially when it came to understanding the company's current, and quite precarious, status. So many business processes were still taking shape, and so many details and features of the software itself were still in flux.

Even looking back on it now, I am still surprised by how many people stuck around, chose to stay with the company rather than jump ship during those early months and years after Amrik left us. I suppose that reflected the bad labor market at the time. There weren't necessarily a lot of jobs for people to jump into. But things were so very tenuous inside the company, for such a long while, that I couldn't help but take it as a sign of people's goodwill toward Amrik that they stayed. Much later, I asked one of Amrik's most loyal employees why he kept working with us.

"You had the opportunity to leave. Why didn't you?"

"I felt I had to stay to help you, Ladeira."

I'm still touched by that sense of commitment and obligation—or, for some people, that act of faith. They didn't want to see the company dissolve and neither did I. Over and over again I told myself, *Together, we will work on sustaining something we believe in.*

I was staying late most days, trying to get acquainted with all the people, projects, and customers and trying to track business processes. At the time I took over, Amrik had around ninety employees, about sixty of whom were working in the office alongside me. Others were scattered throughout the country, helping to implement and troubleshoot software for our biggest customers. Even with all the people and all the moving parts, there were ways in which the work felt a little easier than my day-to-day experience as a high-risk obstetrics nurse. There, I had been making split-second decisions that were quite literally a matter of life or death. But here in the office, I could begin each day with the very general question "What will help the company move forward?" Then I could gather more information, analyze details, and sleep on any preliminary conclusions to see if my attitude about them was any different in the morning. That in itself, the amount of time that I could give to pressing matters, felt like such a luxury.

I was learning a lot from all my conversations with employees, but I still needed a trustworthy sounding board of my own. Thankfully, there was Frederick, to whom I could take any questions and talk them through until I understood them from multiple angles. I could rely on him to be objective and thoughtful, and I knew he wouldn't shy away from telling things as they were. He was about the only person in a management role that I could trust in those early months—and that's probably because I already knew him so well as a member of our extended family.

Often I'd approach Frederick with questions about how to proceed with specific customer demands. "Here's what we're currently doing for this customer . . . But they are demanding that we do this other thing . . . How should I deal with that?" Frederick always offered a candid assessment. I tried not to abuse his generosity. What I really wanted, of course, was the ability to solve issues myself and not need to check in with others. But had Frederick not spent all that time orienting me to the ins and outs of company dealings, I would have struggled mightily to find my footing. I was in survival mode, and Frederick was there to offer life-preserving support.

As I got more acquainted with the lay of the land in the office, I started to think about how there had been subtle changes in Amrik's demeanor in the months leading up to his death. I'd watched him grow increasingly stressed about the company. For one, he was much quieter when we were home together in the evenings. Not wanting to pressure him to talk about it, and sensing that he might prefer some peace and quiet, I would snuggle with him on the couch, resting my head on his chest, and hope that helped a bit. Had I known at that point what I learned in the weeks and months following his death, I might have tried talking directly to him about his distress. Maybe he would have opened up and shared all his worries with me, and then I could have attempted to alleviate some of his discomfort.

What I learned in those early weeks at the office was this: Just two years earlier, at the start of 1997, Amrik had borrowed $3 million from venture capitalists. When he did, he'd agreed to a 50 percent interest rate, with the full amount of the loan plus interest set to be paid back in just two years' time. As part of the arrangement, the VCs had taken a $4 million life insurance policy out on Amrik and assigned a chief operating officer of their own choosing to work at the company and keep them informed of its progress. With the threat of paying the investors on time, the looming uncertainty of Y2K-related computer complications arising during that same period, and what sounded like a disagreement with one of his employees, Amrik was contending with a lot more than I ever could have imagined. Frankly, besides that evening when Amrik told me that Bill was someone who could not be trusted, there was only one other moment of apparent office conflict: Bill had called the house, I'd answered, and Amrik told me he didn't want to take the call. That was it. I understood that something had gone on between them, but Amrik didn't say anything else about it. *They must've had a disagreement,* I'd thought at the time, and let it slide from my mind.

If there were other visible signs of distress, I didn't see them. While Amrik was alive, I treated our personal finances the same way I treated his business—I let Amrik take the lead. Occasionally, I'd say to him, "Hey, I can pay the bills. Why don't you just let me do that for a while."

"No, Ladeira. If I did that, I'd be getting letters saying, 'This bill is overdue, and we are shutting down your service.'" He'd joked with me, but he also wouldn't let me try my hand at it. So Amrik was responsible for all the money. He knew how much was in each of our accounts, and I didn't really keep track of any of it. Now and then, he'd offer a gentle warning. "Be careful how you're spending this week, Ladeira, because I have yet to put more money into that account." For the entirety of our lives together, we'd been very careful with how we spent our money. And the most I ever spent personally was at the nursery, picking up plants and flowers, soil, and other enhancements for the garden.

At no point did I have any reason to believe that Amrik's business could be in any kind of financial trouble. When we moved into our brand-new custom home, I assumed things were going very well at the company. We had lived within our means all the while, never incurring debts that we couldn't easily afford to take on and pay off. Even after Amrik signed his first contract with McDonnell Douglas, the Mercedes that he purchased came from a used car lot.

Once I learned firsthand about all these stressors at the company, I assumed that Amrik had kept quiet about them because he didn't want to burden me and Naveen. I imagined, too, that keeping silent about his mounting worries must have increased his stress fourfold. As a worrier myself, I could understand that protective gesture on Amrik's part. He carried all that worry himself so as not to upset us in any way. That was one of the ways he showed his love.

Of course, when Amrik died, all that worry transferred over to me.

I learned about Amrik's debt from a conversation with the VCs themselves. During the week after Amrik died—when Naveen and I were at home, trying to make sense of what had just happened and set arrangements for Amrik's funeral—the team of VCs had been secretly meeting to determine the fate of the company, on the assumption that it was now entirely within their rights to do so.

By the time I appeared at the office—the following Monday—the VCs were deep in the throes of devising their own behind-the-scenes plan for a company takeover. That plan relied on getting rid of me. I'm surprised it took as many weeks as it did before they told me what they'd been plotting since the early hours after Amrik's death. I suppose they needed to have all their paperwork in order.

Nick, the company's treasurer, attended the closed meeting with me when the VCs made their announcement. "Ladeira," they said, "you will no longer be the CEO of this company." For them, it was that simple. There were no formalities, no documents to sign, nor any discernable process. Just an impromptu-seeming, semiprivate meeting during which they shared with me and Nick news they clearly assumed I should have expected to hear. There was no conversation about my intentions, my sense of Amrik's wishes, my ability or inability to step into the CEO role, or the optics of having an obstetrics nurse at the helm of a software company. None of that. Just an announcement that I was expected to obey.

Nick tried to ease the blow by inquiring, "Why don't you help her out and at least let her work at something here within the company?"

They looked incredulous.

It wasn't until a meeting they held shortly afterward—a meeting to which, of course, I hadn't been invited and about which I hadn't been informed ahead of time—that the company's lawyer, Jacob, offered up the following conundrum for their consideration: "Exactly how are you going to get rid of Ladeira when she owns 85 percent of the company?"

I appreciated Jacob's challenge to the VCs and his willingness to assure me that they couldn't just kick me to the curb, but if it looked to any of us like they backed off after that meeting, their hesitation was short-lived. Since they couldn't oust me as easily as they'd anticipated, they came for their money instead.

It was January 1999—not even a full two months after we lost Amrik—when they made their second announcement to me.

"You owe us $6 million."

They'd already received $4 million from their life insurance policy on Amrik. But the loan for $3 million plus interest had come due. I suppose I should have felt thankful that Amrik hadn't given them shares in the company and had only managed to be millions of dollars in debt from a loan. As I understood it, if he'd given them shares, they would have had the power to boot me out, even though I still would have had majority ownership. But Amrik had made a debt financing arrangement, and so the VCs' only legal move at this point was to demand immediate repayment.

As Jacob put it to me, if they couldn't get rid of me outright, they were going to do everything they could to make it impossible for me to stay. "Don't worry," their appointed chief operating officer had started telling some other employees, "she'll be out in another month, and then I'll be in charge."

I viewed the VCs' demand for immediate repayment on their loan not only as a threat to the company—and a way of taking control of it that bypassed the matter of shareholder power—but also as a threat to me and Naveen personally. On both counts, my first instinct had been to panic.

How am I going to pay back all that money?

The VCs were at my throat, wanting access to everything we had—Amrik's personal life insurance money, our bank accounts, the house mortgage.

My God, they are going to destroy us.

My second instinct was not to let anyone see my panic, especially Naveen. I researched our financial options, all the while barely able to breathe at the thought of what could result. Naveen was happy in his high school and in our new home. I had to figure out how to keep Amrik's company from being destroyed and keep me and Naveen from being thrown out on the street. I supposed that if it was necessary, we could liquidate the company in a fire sale.

Many nights, as I tried to fall asleep, I'd find myself thinking about when Naveen was just a boy. I'd take him out to the yard with me so that I could teach him how to plant seeds in the garden. I remembered the excitement in his expression each time he witnessed the sprouted seedlings. The first year we gardened together, several of the seeds he'd planted didn't take. But I so much wanted to make him happy that I went out and bought seedlings, then planted them where he'd placed his seeds—so it looked as if they'd naturally sprouted up from the ground.

What I was certain of now, as then, is that I would do anything to protect Naveen and to make him happy. Amrik had started cultivating a legacy for Naveen. I would have to make sure that the seeds he'd planted would bear fruit.

CHAPTER 7

Amrik and I met during the summer of 1971, just after my first year at nursing school in Exeter. My girlfriends and I had gone out to a local pub to celebrate completing our exams. In those days, all the girls would dance together to the blaring disco music, while the boys milled around the edges of the dance floor, watching to determine which girls they wanted to ask for a dance. Eventually, couples would pair off when a boy approached a girl by tapping her on the shoulder to get her attention. Amrik tapped me on the shoulder that evening, and we started dancing together. When he offered to buy me a drink, I agreed and asked for a rum and Coke. He came back to the dance floor with a drink in each hand. When I tasted mine, I could tell immediately that it was just a Coke.

He was deeply apologetic about it. "I'm so sorry. The bartender must not have heard me correctly!" Together, we enjoyed our Cokes, danced, and talked throughout the rest of the evening.

As we talked, I learned that he had just finished his first year at an engineering program in Plymouth—about an hour away from Exeter by train. Before moving to England to attend school and live close to one of his older brothers, Amrik had wanted to become a Bollywood actor. He'd grown up in the countryside in India where, as a boy, he'd charmed all his neighbors into investing to help him start a chicken farm. Eventually, his desire to be in movies grew so strong that one day, without telling anyone, he hopped a passenger train to Bombay, avoiding paying a fare throughout the entire trip by climbing up on top of the train each time the ticket taker was set to pass by.

Once in Bollywood, Amrik got some official headshots taken and was quickly selected for a leading role in a film. Even though he'd arrived in Bollywood with no connections in the industry and knowing no one there, he was a very handsome and charismatic man. The speed with which he'd been scooped up by the film industry hadn't surprised me. When the funding for the project didn't materialize and it seemed that Amrik would be stranded in Bombay without work, his parents called on his brother Rohit to invite Amrik to England so that he could pursue a more reliable career path. Then they called on his eldest brother, Mohit—himself an engineering professor in America—to help convince Amrik that it was time to get a university degree. All the brothers were expected to take care of one another, help each other succeed. Mohit had gotten a scholarship in the army. Then he'd helped Rohit travel to England to study and begin a teaching career. And now it was Rohit's turn to help Amrik—in this case, to lure him away from Bombay before he started taking too seriously his desire to become a movie star.

Amrik received scholarships to fund his studies at Plymouth. Then, only weeks after he started classes toward earning an engineering degree, he received word that the movie's funding had come through and the team wanted him to return to Bombay to begin production. What surprised me was hearing Amrik talk about how he analyzed the situation and decided that returning to Bombay to take a chance on a film career would be too dangerous. He turned down the offer and instead fully engaged with his new plan to become an engineer. In summers, he came to Exeter to work in one of the local pubs and earn extra money.

When we left the pub that night, Amrik walked with the group of us girls back to our nursing residence hall and asked if he could see me again. I didn't give him my number—frankly, I don't remember saying anything at all in direct answer to his query. He was a really handsome guy, and that was one of the reasons I didn't want to date him. How could a person be so intelligent, so mature, and so physically appealing at the same time? I was suspicious of this incongruity from the start, almost determined to find a significant flaw that would make him seem more average.

Though I hadn't shared my contact information, Amrik figured out how to get in touch with me. So I saw him again, several times as a matter of fact, throughout that summer. And when the following school year got underway, he started traveling by train once a month to come visit me in Exeter. We would go for walks or meet in the park and sit under a tree, reading to each other. I'd pack us sandwiches for lunch, we'd enjoy an afternoon picnic, then Amrik would take the train back to Plymouth at the end of the day.

When Naveen was about six or seven years old, one of his school assignments was to write about how his mother and father first met. I still have the sheet of paper on which Naveen wrote: My mother went to a nightclub to have fun. My father went to the same nightclub to meet a girl.

Years later, Amrik would admit to me that he'd just ordered Coke that night when he introduced himself to me on the dance floor. He couldn't afford to add in the rum. His schooling was funded entirely by scholarships and grants, and that money he earned in the summertime was intended to help him through the following school year. Not knowing or recognizing these details in the early months of our courtship, I failed to realize that some of our dates—especially the ones where he took me out for dinner—were a true strain on his finances. Here was this young man counting his pennies, and there I was ordering quite a lot of food and not even finishing it. If Amrik took me to a Chinese restaurant, I'd order a full table's worth of food: fried rice, chow mein, a meat dish, drinks, dessert. Whatever I didn't finish, I'd leave on the table, assuming that if I were to take the leftovers and place them in the communal fridge of the residence I shared with the other nursing students, they'd get stolen before I could enjoy them again.

After we were married, Amrik admitted his amazement at my food orders. "You didn't even eat! You barely touched the food!" The poor man would have to assess his pocketbook after each dinner date, wondering how much he would still have left and how to make it last throughout the remainder of the academic year.

Smart, handsome, gracious, and compelling as Amrik was—precisely because he was all these things—I couldn't bring myself to trust him. I thought about the doctors around whom we nurses trained and remembered hearing one of them bragging to a group of others that he "had the first-year nurses for breakfast, the second-years for lunch, and the third-years for dinner." Several of the nurses in training accepted the assumption he was making: that because he was a man with a good profession, we young women were supposed to be impressed and agreeable when asked out on dates. I was a wise girl. And I wasn't going to go on a date with him just to have fun. So when he propositioned me, I looked him in the eye and said, "I'm a first-year nurse! No, no, no, no, no. I don't want to be your breakfast, lunch, or dinner." I'd been surprised that answering him like that had earned me some respect. At the very least, it had earned me a spot on his "just leave that one alone" list.

In addition to remembering not to hang myself with all the rope I'd been given, I'd kept several additional bits of advice from my father top of mind, one of which was: "You can never trust a person 100 percent. Always be on the lookout for disappointment. And don't *ever* trust any guys from India." My father shared that last bit of advice knowing full well that nearly half the population of Trinidad was of Indian descent. Still, he intended to draw a clear distinction between Indo-Trinidadian and Indian men. Of the latter, he clarified: "They will happily date you, but ultimately they will listen to and obey their parents, who usually have already picked out someone for them to marry."

I took that advice seriously and had already seen the evidence with my own eyes: There were a number of Indian doctors working at the hospital who dated the nurses, only to go back to India to marry someone else. On at least one occasion, I went so far as to share my suspicion directly with Amrik: "For all I know, you already have a wife in India! My father told me to watch out for Indian men and never to get involved with them. You'll date me and then leave me high and dry."

Amrik had responded by showing me his passport to convince me that, at the very least, I should believe he was a single man. He wanted to offer material proof that he was an honest person, that not every Indian man was as I'd assumed them all to be.

It was a sweet gesture, if not entirely convincing.

The more interest Amrik showed in pursuing a relationship with me, the more I reminded myself that I had traveled to England to advance my own opportunities in this world and make my way independently in my chosen career. I didn't want to get hurt by a man who—even if he didn't think he would—could possibly return to India and marry a woman his parents had already hand selected for him.

My instinct to protect myself didn't arise just as a result of the words my father spoke to me before I left home to study in England. Growing up in Trinidad, I'd developed a serious mistrust of other people. Or rather, I'd decided it was a very realistic approach to withhold that trust until people proved themselves trustworthy. Even as a young girl, I was committed to not trusting anyone 100 percent. I'd listened to people in the pub gossiping and telling tall tales about their families and their lives; I'd seen people promise to pay and then run out on their tabs; I'd received unwanted attention from older, married men interested in dating me. Even my own father . . . I suspected that at some point when I was very young, he'd hurt my mother in such a way that she no longer trusted him all that much. My father had been very good to us kids, but I'd also overheard my mother talking with others about dishonesty in their relationship. That detail had planted itself in the back of my mind. All the more reason, I suppose, to follow his advice: You shouldn't trust anyone 100 percent, not even the people you would hope to be able to trust the most.

In my experience, there were a lot of dishonest people around me when I was growing up, and that necessitated being very careful with everyone. I doubted everything that came out of a person's mouth until it could be satisfactorily proved. Then, after traveling to England from a third-world country, I'd come to rely on that approach for the sake of my own safety. I needed to be able to protect myself, and I believed that a cautious approach to everyone I met would pay off well.

Amrik's inclinations, by contrast, seemed so strange to me—the minute he met a person, he was so sincere and believed everything anyone said to him! Naveen is just like his father in this way. To this day, it upsets Naveen that I always begin from a place of distrust.

The funny thing about Amrik was that the more I discouraged him, the more he pursued me. I remember agreeing to meet him one afternoon at two and then deciding last minute that I wasn't going to show up. But Amrik was clever. He knew by then that if I wasn't showing up to meet him, I was likely to go visit my sister Hana. He even knew the route that I was likely to take. When I arrived at Hana and Robin's place, there was Amrik, sitting on a bench, waiting for me with a big smile across his face. So I suggested he meet Hana, half figuring that he would run from the opportunity. If that was a test, he passed it masterfully. Hana genuinely liked him, and eventually, when he met them, so did all my family. I kept looking for ways to find fault with him, and he kept being his patient and respectful self. Later on, I'd learn that he even wrote a letter to my father expressing his interest in me and, indirectly, asking permission for us to date one another. My niece said they passed the letter around to all the family. My father's response? "He seems like a nice guy."

Even after we were married, we'd travel to Trinidad every two years or so. Each visit, the whole of my family clearly loved having Amrik around. He was a good man, and even I had to acknowledge that he knew how to blend with the different members of my family. Not only did they appreciate that he was brilliant and charming, but they also seemed to celebrate that my marrying someone from India was like reconnecting with and honoring our family's roots.

Nevertheless, several factors—the difficulty of fending for myself in a foreign country, the need to safeguard my future, and old habits developed in childhood—became real obstacles to exploring my true feelings for Amrik. I wanted a friendship, and I wanted to finish my studies and return to Trinidad. I'm not sure when it was or precisely what triggered it, but at the end of one of our dates, I announced this to Amrik outright: "I don't want to get involved in a serious relationship. I just don't want to date you anymore." In one sense, I'd surprised myself by speaking precisely those words; in another, they'd seemed to suit the situation perfectly.

When I saw Amrik's reaction, the stunned and injured expression on his face as he turned to walk away after my pronouncement, I felt a rush of sadness well up in me. Within seconds, I was calling after him: "No, no! It's okay. You can call on me. I'll see you tomorrow, okay?"

Like that, Amrik's status shifted from "casual friend" to "person I want to date seriously." For the first time, I thought to myself, *This man really likes me and wants to get to know me better.*

It's funny to me the way people talk about falling in love— the heart fluttering, the desire to see and be with another person all the time. The way love gets talked about makes me wonder if such a thing even exists. The way I see it, what happens with love is that you get used to a person and to your relationship with them; you grow comfortable being together.

And hadn't I seen quite the opposite happen to Hana, who didn't seem to have thought about the future she might have with Robin? I'd struggled to make sense of her decision to be with him. No Trinidadian man would ever have been good enough for her, no matter his education, looks, good job, or good standing in the community. Better she get involved with a hopeless loser in England, a man no other woman in our entire family would ever dream of marrying.

I'd been a firsthand witness to Hana's transformation. She worked at a good government-backed organization and paid the mortgage on their house, and all my brother-in-law did was go to his airport job, come home, eat the dinner that Hana had prepared, and then head out to one of the local pubs for an evening of drinking. That was the entirety of his life.

On my days off, I would often go over to Hana's for dinner. She'd realized relatively early on that she'd made an error choosing Robin and would complain to me about him. "Leave him!" I'd encourage her. But Hana was a strange bird in her own right. She convinced herself that she must have done something terrible in a past life, something that led her to marry this person. She felt obligated to stay with him to right whatever wrong she'd committed.

I couldn't get that idea out of her head. "If you're unhappy, leave. Just. Leave. Him. Nobody will think twice about it. You'll find someone better in a heartbeat!"

Hana could not tell a lie or hold back information, so of course she told Robin that I'd encouraged her to leave him. The first few times I visited them after she shared with him my opinion, I kept thinking, *This guy knows what I think about him!* It didn't take long, though, before I also thought, *That's his problem.*

But then Hana became a different person. She stopped taking care of herself. She no longer dressed attractively. Her whole demeanor changed, and she lived a secluded and very quiet life. I felt she was making herself more and more like Robin. When she visited Trinidad, people no longer recognized her as the same person they'd known only a handful of years before. She was completely different, and until the day she died I never stopped thinking what a shame it was that she'd chosen a life that drained her of her own liveliness and joy. And I'd never stop detesting Robin for the role he played in her transformation.

Without question, Hana's situation influenced my thinking about potential life mates. *Look what happens when you marry the wrong person,* I would think to myself. Not me. I was going to make sure that what happened to Hana wouldn't also happen to me. I felt convinced that I needed a guy who would graduate into a successful career. I knew Amrik was ambitious, and I knew he wanted to start his own business at some point. I wanted a smart and ambitious guy, someone who would make our lives better, and someone who would encourage me to expand my horizons, have my own career, become the best version of myself.

That's why I took a more practical approach to my relationship with Amrik and was pleased that I could picture our future: If we were to get more involved and each of us continued along our chosen career paths, we'd both become professionals living a good, grounded life together. We would avoid the hardships of worrying about how to make ends meet and living paycheck to paycheck. Instead, I pictured us having kids and me being able to stay home with them—maybe work part-time—knowing that if I did that, we would still be financially comfortable.

I hadn't come to Exeter to find a mate. I wasn't looking to fall in love. And what I wanted, ultimately, was to be with someone whose trajectory and personality suggested that together we could improve our lot, deepen our quality of life. Of course, Amrik was very bright—brilliant, really, and steady. These details further convinced me to give a serious relationship with him a try.

I decided that I would proceed while remaining cautious—firmly committed to making sure that I didn't fall into any traps, end up hurt, or have my own chances at a better life derailed. But I would also make space for Amrik.

Of course, both of us were still students without much money. I did my best to save what I could, because I knew I needed to support myself no matter what happened. My mother had always told us children, "Always, always save for a rainy day. If you get ten dollars, save five of them." If from my father's advice I'd developed a staunch practicality about relationships, from my mother's advice I'd developed a firm pragmatism about finances. To this very day, I watch how I spend money. I live within my means, so that in case of emergency, I won't need to depend on anybody.

CHAPTER 8

A couple of months after our relationship grew more serious, I received a phone call from Amrik canceling, at the last minute, a weekend visit we had planned. He was calling from a phone booth.

"Hey, Ladeira. You know where I am?"

"On your way here?"

"Well, my brother has taken me to London to meet the family of a girl that he wants me to marry. He says the family is offering a large dowry." He was cheery in his usual way.

"Oh." I paused. And then added, "I see."

I wasn't angry. Instead, I thought my practical thoughts.

Well, we were just dating. I am doing very well in my studies. I have my career to think of.

There will be other people.

If this is going to continue, it will, and if not, it will not.

To which I added: *I knew this would happen.*

Amrik's brother Rohit didn't like me one bit and had not hesitated to express his dissatisfaction with our dating. At our very first introduction, he'd made a sidewise comment: "I didn't think Black people had straight hair."

"Your brother has a very poor understanding of geography," I'd replied, keeping my eyes focused on Amrik.

Now, just as Amrik and I were growing closer, Rohit had gone and arranged for Amrik to be introduced to a family in London that could offer a big dowry and was more than ready to treat Amrik like a king.

Amrik and I didn't speak any more about the trip in the time that passed between the date he'd missed and the next time he visited.

When we saw one another again, I began with a simple question. "So, how did it go in London?"

"My brother is mad with me because I told him I was not interested in this arrangement."

I found that satisfactory. We dropped the subject, and Amrik continued to pursue his relationship with me.

That might have been a moment when I turned away—cynically believing that by my very own experience, I'd proved the truth and value of my father's words and my worst expectations. But I understood it differently—this very gesture was part of what made Amrik different from other Indian men. He wanted to make his own decisions rather than let his family choose for him. If he met someone he liked, he was going to pursue that person. Already in life, he hadn't behaved like a traditional Indian guy. He'd always wanted to leave India and see the world; even venturing to Bollywood was a way of leaving behind more traditional roots. And though his family was Sikh, Amrik had bucked the religious doctrine that prohibited cutting off his hair. Granted, after he cut his hair short, he continued wearing a turban so that his parents wouldn't notice. Nevertheless, he'd wanted more. More than that, he didn't seem at all to mind being different.

As I saw it, disinterest in the potential mate his brother hand selected for him was thoroughly consistent with Amrik's personality. He didn't want to date a typical Indian girl. Instead, he wanted to pursue someone like me.

I finished my degree a year before Amrik completed his. Most of the girls in my class were continuing on with their schooling to secure a specialized degree, and I was no exception. For me, there was an additional motivator: If I lost my student status in England, I would have to return to Trinidad. So I decided to specialize in midwifery, which allowed me to remain in the country and move to Plymouth, so that Amrik and I could live in the same place.

Amrik was the one who did all the planning in our relationship. It was he who'd suggested, "You can come to Plymouth and study midwifery, and we can get married." That was exactly what we did.

Of course, we had to get settled in our apartment before hosting our wedding reception there. We'd found a little place on the second floor of a three-story walk-up, with other renters living above and below us. When we moved in, the lawn in front of the flat was as tall as me; every time I walked through it, I would worry that I might be attacked by snakes, or that there might even be a whole human person hiding in the grass, ready to pounce. The first housekeeping action I took was to rent a lawn mower. After I cut it all down, our landlord thought that the lawn looked so good, he offered us a rebate on our rent. So long as I kept cutting the lawn, we would enjoy the reduced rate.

Amrik and I married in the summer of 1973, about two years after we'd met.

We went to the registry office on a Friday, then hosted a reception in our apartment on Saturday for all our school friends—just in time for me to begin coursework on Monday.

Hana came alone to the reception. Still smarting from having Amrik turn down the bride and dowry he'd selected,

Rohit refused to celebrate our wedding with us. Unlike Rohit, Amrik's parents and other family members sent their blessings and well-wishes; so long as Amrik was happy with his marriage, they were happy too. The same was true for my parents and siblings.

In all, getting married and celebrating at home with friends cost us about ten pounds. The parents of one of Amrik's school friends owned a local pub and sent over some champagne to mark the occasion; that was my first taste of the fizzy drink. We ordered a keg of beer, and everyone else brought a bit of food—sandwiches, snacks, vegetables, and for dessert, a good friend had made little Jell-O cups, each with a dollop of crème and a cherry on top. It was such a happy occasion; everyone stayed late and thoroughly enjoyed themselves. The next day, when Amrik went to check the keg, there was just enough beer left to fill a single glass. Everyone had drunk as much as they wanted, and we'd made it through the evening without exhausting our supply. Everything had worked out perfectly.

When he graduated the following year with his engineering degree, Amrik was the only student in the entire university to have earned First-Class Honors. First-Class Honors were a rare achievement at the time, and Amrik had ranked first among those receiving that top honor. Since he didn't have any interest in participating in the graduation ceremony, he'd missed out on receiving that honor in public. Frankly, I would have enjoyed seeing him exalted among his peers.

Throughout the entirety of Amrik's studies, there'd been a fellow classmate of his who was always trying to outrank him on exams. Amrik studied, did well, and never felt he was in competition with anyone. But this other student was locked in competition with Amrik, challenging himself to beat Amrik at every turn. To me, it seemed as if that other student, an Englishman, couldn't believe that a handsome man from India could continuously outrank him. When we met this fellow in the street a few weeks after graduation, he approached Amrik with a sour face. "I tried so very hard to compete with you, but I guess I could not."

Amrik and I giggled after he went on his way.

Much later on, when Naveen was in grade school, one of his classmates would take up the same attitude. Naveen would ace his tests without much effort, while that poor other boy was locked into some sort of imaginary competition, nearly a feud, with him. I remember dropping Naveen off at school one morning and seeing this other boy walking just ahead of us, mumbling—not entirely to himself—"Gotta beat Naveen. Gotta beat Naveen" as he passed through the entrance.

To this day, I'm still surprised by the ways that Naveen is so much like his father—intelligent, compelling, bighearted, trusting, and easy to talk to. Nearly everyone who has ever met either of them has adored them, except for a very few who, at their own expense, imagined themselves a fair rival.

CHAPTER 9

Immediately after moving to England, I regularly sent money home every month to pay back my mother for the plane ticket my father had insisted she purchase for me. After some time, Amrik suggested I not continue worrying about the ticket, and I agreed to stop the monthly payments. But for holidays and birthdays, I still sent what money I could home to my family.

Our whole group of friends in England had been established through the men. They were all engineers, all largely from India, and even though they did not all attend university together, we couples somehow found one another. Amrik was the youngest of the group, and after he graduated, one of our friends helped him get his first job. We were a tight-knit group, all about the same age, all finding our way.

Once I graduated from the midwifery program, I noticed that I was finally feeling used to the lifestyle in England and comfortable with my role at work. But Amrik, who was never satisfied, wanted us to move to Canada so that he could attend graduate school there, and he already had his eye on us moving more permanently to the United States, where his brothers Mohit and Rahul lived. Our whole group of friends essentially decided to move together to Canada, with a goal of eventually establishing permanent residence in the US. Amrik was all the more motivated by the fact that Mohit was doing very well in the US. So he applied for and earned a scholarship to complete his master's degree in Canada.

When he decided this, I was working as an assistant head nurse, in charge of the whole department. I had a great position; I didn't much want to relocate to Canada, and I was upset with Amrik for making a unilateral decision that we needed to leave England right then. I'd already uprooted my life once. I'd left Trinidad, made my way in England, and now he wanted to uproot me from all that I'd earned in this new life so that we could start all over again in another country. When I married Amrik, I knew that I would never move back to Trinidad. I understood that he had bigger plans. But that didn't make me any less annoyed with his rush to transition our lives so quickly.

Had Amrik only been concerned about himself, I would have been terribly angry, maybe even considered not accompanying him. But he was extremely encouraging: "You may have to go to school for a year or so, Ladeira, to get familiar with the way the Canadians and Americans do things, but just think how much better your life, and our lives, will be!"

Amrik's attitude was that we would do what we needed to do to move our lives forward. The entire group of friends seemed to agree, and when it came time, every couple moved to Ottawa. We all lived in the same area and did what we could to support one another on our journeys.

Of course, what we needed most when we got to Canada was money, and we needed it quite desperately. Amrik's scholarship paid for rent and food, and nothing else. At the time, the country seemed to have a surplus of nurses, all needing jobs, and although I had excellent credentials and experience, what I no longer had was a functional RN license. In other words, until I rewrote my board exams in-country, I couldn't even compete for any of the jobs for which I was qualified.

To make ends meet, I applied for work at a nursing home and picked up a job as an aide, earning $3.65 an hour. I will never forget that. The job brought in money and helped us get by, but it was not at all easy to have shifted from being in charge of a department—entrusted with matters of life and death and the management of a team of nurses—only to find my duties restricted to feeding patients and recording vital signs.

Within my first few months working at the home, there was an emergency situation—a patient with a dangerous bowel obstruction—during which I was the only person around who could identify the emergency and clarify what needed to be done. That opportunity to prove what I knew and save a life earned me a certain respect among my colleagues, but I still needed to pass the boards to practice nursing at the level I had been accustomed to. Until then, I would bide my time in the old people's home as the unofficial emergency consultant: the person that everyone turned to, asking, "What do you think?" Most of the nurses there had never worked in a general hospital; they'd simply landed those jobs right after they graduated.

To become qualified to take the board exams in Canada, I had to acquire additional educational credits; courses in psychiatry, for example, were part of the standard curriculum in both Canada and the US but hadn't been required in England. Eventually, I took my boards, my license went through, and I found a job more appropriate to my skills and training.

Besides our close group of friends, we also were close with Mohit, who was a full fifteen years Amrik's senior and treated Amrik almost as a son. Mohit had encouraged Amrik to go to England all those years ago and had contributed to paying for Amrik's food and other essentials during his time as a student. Over the years, the two of them remained very close, and when we moved to Canada we visited with Mohit and his family on the regular, about four times a year. That was a period during which Mohit's support for Amrik extended also to me. Mohit would come up from New Jersey to drive me to interviews for nursing jobs. He did whatever he could to help out.

I'd sensed that Mohit's wife, Dina, never much liked me. Later on, Amrik would tell me a story about how Dina hadn't liked me from the start—a circumstance to which I'd done nothing to contribute except to have become Amrik's wife.

You see, I'd married the man she thought she would be promised to. Her family and Amrik's family in India were closely tied together. Often, when that's the case, the families intertwine: The eldest son of one family would marry the eldest daughter from the other, then the eldest son's brothers would likely partner with the remaining girls. Dina always had her eye on Amrik, and she'd liked him since they were just children.

Her older sister had been promised to Mohit, but she didn't want to marry him and found her own way of escaping the arrangement. But because her parents had promised Mohit he'd marry within the family, the next daughter in line was Dina. She was fourteen years younger than Mohit and never seemed to get over the fact that she'd imagined her future with Amrik. In those early years, her feelings hadn't seemed to affect the family dynamic, and we shared good times whenever we visited.

Amrik and I got by, and when he finished his degree, he was ready to make that final international move to the US. This time, our group of close friends who had all traveled to Ottawa was not able to stay together. Nearly everyone moved to the US, but we all found ourselves settling in states far apart from one another. From that point forward, our friendships would be sustained by annual trips—sometimes a cruise, sometimes meeting up to explore a part of the country new to us all.

The irony of Amrik's plan to enter the US was that he

ended up having to rely on me to get in. At that time, most of the people from India who lived in America were doctors, lawyers, engineers—all relatively prestigious careers. Amrik applied for US visas for us, but then he received a letter notifying him that the US had plenty of engineers. What that country didn't have enough of at the time, however, was nurses. This meant that I would have to be the primary visa applicant instead of Amrik. After all my effort to make good on our situation in Canada and find work that would help us survive, I took some pleasure in that detail.

To this day, I believe that being a nurse has helped me out a lot in life. Every job I interviewed for, I got. In each country, I was able immediately to find a job that would at least help with our finances, if not advance them. When we moved from Canada to Houston, Texas, I easily found employment in high-risk obstetrics. Amrik was hired at Texas Instruments, and we both finally felt that we had arrived. Coming to the US had been Amrik's sole focus, and now here we were. To my surprise, there was a pace to the time we spent in Houston that I very much enjoyed. But there was one experience that stuck with me, even influenced decisions I made much later, when it became my responsibility to lead Amrik's business in his absence.

Quite simply, what happened was that a freshly graduated young nurse reported me to our supervisor for an infraction.

Of course, what happened was more complicated than that. I had taken it upon myself to take quick and decisive action to achieve a good outcome for one of our patients. I knew what the situation required, and instead of pausing to phone the doctor, describe the complication, and spend precious seconds waiting for his permission to act, I chose to address it directly. I knew what I was doing, knew what the doctor would say to me, and made the decision to act first and call him afterward to report what I'd done.

When the freshly minted nurse saw this, she immediately reported me for not calling the doctor before acting. The charge nurse and I had a fine follow-up conversation. She reminded me of the protocol about calling the doctor, and I pointed out that while I understood the need to call the doctor, I also both didn't want a patient to die and knew just what to do to prevent that from happening. This doctor and I had gone through the same experience with several other patients prior to this event. I had made a decision not to observe protocol in this instance to more quickly engage in lifesaving activity.

The matter ended there, but I couldn't get over the fact that a newly graduated nurse had seen fit to report me before talking with me and inquiring about my reasons. I wondered if she'd done so simply to gain brownie points. So I sought her out one day shortly thereafter and told her what I thought of her decision: "Let me tell you, the best way to gain brownie points is to do your work and do it to the best of your ability— not to run to the charge nurse, especially not without having all the information about the situation. The charge nurse won't respect you for that. You cannot do that to move ahead."

Honestly, I didn't know what the charge nurse would respect. But I felt a deep conviction that each of us deserved the opportunity to explain our actions—even receive mentoring if that was determined necessary. More than once in my tenure overseeing Amrik's business, I would discover employees who believed that they could get ahead by sabotaging one another or by ingratiating themselves to those in charge. I think that's why I spent so much time talking with everyone at the office. I wanted to be sure that I had the fullest understanding of what was going on and that, together, we could make sense of how to find a way forward. As a result, rarely was there a time when it seemed to me that someone's infraction qualified them for reprimand or other official action, let alone being let go.

CHAPTER 10

I continued spending my days at the office, learning everything I could and doing my best to monitor the flow of money in and out, make sure that employees had what they needed to be successful in their jobs, and improve—or at least maintain—morale. That last item turned out to be the most consuming of the three goals I'd set myself.

Ted, our head of research and development, remained an obstacle, focusing most of his energy on being critical of me whenever he could identify an opportunity. Thankfully, his team of engineers was both in good shape and tended to stay out of office politics. They were brilliant at product development and refinement, and very invested in making the software a success. I appreciated them for that, especially since that was an aspect of our work in which I would have needed specific, technical knowledge to fully understand their efforts. It was good that as a group they were kind and generally supportive of my leadership.

So far as I was concerned, the real trouble with Ted was not his machinations in relation to me. Instead, my true concern was that, though Amrik had put him in charge of a team, he was simply no good at managing people. At best, he was interested in being everyone's friend. He made excuses when people didn't turn their work in on schedule, and he avoided attending to any of his responsibilities that were not directly focused on enhancing the product itself. The consequences were problematic. Once, when I stopped at his office to ask about one of his team members, who had been out for a week after undergoing major surgery, Ted stared at me, perplexed. I was shocked to learn that he was utterly unaware of either the surgery or his teammate's extended absence.

This is what happens, I did not say to him out loud, *when you spend so much time and energy being angry that I'm CEO and you're not.*

Not all of Ted's fussing at me was benign. Occasionally he was able to convince other managers to take up his point of view and act on it. I could see that he had been influencing Mark, our head of sales, encouraging him to disregard my efforts to understand how his team worked. And all too often, Ted's attempts to push my buttons occurred before an audience of fellow colleagues. I'd made explicit policy of two practices I'd instituted when I got started as CEO: First, I regularly made the rounds, saying hello to employees to find out how they were doing and what they needed, and to reiterate to them that I would make myself available whenever they wished to address any issue with me directly. Second, and in conjunction with that first rule, I insisted on having an open-door policy. The open-door policy wasn't just about making myself available when someone wanted to talk. It was also a reflection of my belief that it was possible to de-escalate conflicts, even prevent them, and to find practical solutions to whatever problems employees brought to my attention.

When an employee would take advantage of my open-door policy, I made sure to keep confidential the official content of our conversation. I wanted everyone to have a fair chance. To me, one of the most important things I could do was to never hold against anyone something they had the courage to come talk to me about. When those conversations did occur, I made a concerted effort to be direct in my responses. I would tell employees my feelings about whatever they'd shared, and then I would do my best to clarify what I would like to see done to resolve the issue they were facing. I firmly disagreed with the idea that one's human resources file needed to contain a detailed account of every meeting, every conversation. Talk with people? Yes, absolutely. Develop specific plans for improvement? Yes. But start a file to make permanent and potentially detrimental something that was shared in confidence that an employee wants to improve? For better or worse, I was deeply opposed.

I learned from the little group of employees who were eager to keep me informed about goings-on at the office that the first of those policies—being sure that I circulated among employees and asked how they were doing—was referred to by Ted as "Ladeira doing her bed checks." It's true that looking in on employees was one of the ways that my training as a nurse had proven beneficial in the office: I was good at reading people and sensing what they needed, and talking with them individually helped me know better how I might help them. But Ted took what I considered a highly developed skill and turned it against me, making me seem controlling instead of interested or concerned. His framing made it seem as if I was merely showing up to check for signs of life—or worse, lurking in doorways with a checklist, concerned only with making a note of which people were sitting upright at their desks, appearing to do their jobs.

It didn't help that besides the personal visits and the open-door policy, I had no other way to assess what Ted and his department were doing. Whenever I asked Ted to report on his team's progress and needs, he often grew defensive and summarily dismissed me: "Ladeira, it's none of your business how I'm managing my people. Rest assured, I'm doing everything that needs to be done, and I certainly don't need to explain myself to *you!*"

I took only the slightest bit of solace in the fact that whatever Bill said to Ted also went in one ear and out the other.

Bill was another one who seemed unable to adjust to my role as owner. It took me some time to figure out the right approach, but on one occasion, after I felt he'd crossed a line, I got fed up and made my position clear. One of the consequences of employees being generally afraid of Bill was that they started seeking me out as a buffer against his seeming abuses of power.

On one occasion, an employee who had been with the company for just under a month approached Bill with a request for a $5,000 personal loan—a bold move, for certain, and one I might have imagined would be summarily dismissed. But in response, Bill made an even bolder move, instructing our accountant to produce the $5,000.

The accountant refused to do so until I approved.

Bill's approach was just as I might have anticipated: "Ladeira," he said, storming into my office, "I am the president of this company, and I told him to write a check!"

There was only one sensible response: "Bill, I am the owner of this company, and I say no!"

Other conflicts were less confrontational, such as when Vanessa, who took charge of reviewing expense reports, started quietly leaving Bill's paperwork on my desk. I'd seen him curse at her before—and she certainly had no hesitation about cursing right back at him—so I was not at all surprised when she shared these samples of his misuse of company funds. I understood that someone needed to stand up to him and that it shouldn't be the responsibility of people in positions with less power than his to take up that task. From the pages Vanessa left on my desk, and from my knowledge of the schedule of client visits, it was clear that many of the expenses Bill was claiming as work related were fraudulent. Amrik had pointed out Bill's abuse of company funds when he traveled with his mistress, but now I could see that Bill was just visiting our local pubs in the evenings and charging drinks and meals to the company.

It was my job to approach him, which I did on several occasions over a relatively short period of time. First: "Bill, why are we getting expense reports from you on weeks when we've had no customers? If you met with clients, please do let us know exactly who, as the form requires." And then, "Bill, I need to talk with you about some expense reports. I've noticed that every day for the past several weeks you've been going out drinking after work. But there haven't been any customers in town for meetings. Why are you abusing company funds?" And so on from there.

Rarely did Bill ever respond directly to my inquiries. Even when he was in the same room as me, looking me in the eye as I pointed out reporting discrepancies, he would often simply remain silent or storm out of the office—sometimes both.

Until one afternoon when I called him into my office. "We cannot be spending money unnecessarily, Bill. That includes going out and charging drinks to your company card every evening. Let me be clear: It is not acceptable to use company funds for your personal enjoyment."

As I might have expected from his behavior toward others, he started cursing at me. The thing is, I hadn't expected it. He'd always found a way to be either silent or curt with me, never violent.

I raised my voice as loud as I could without shouting: "Bill, my husband would never be disrespectful to your wife. And I don't expect you to be disrespectful to me. Now get out of my office!"

Just like that, I'd shocked myself twice over. First, I hadn't expected to rely on my position as Amrik's wife in rebuking Bill. And second, that was the first time I'd referred to Amrik's office as my own.

Apparently, I'd also shocked the employees who were within earshot of our conversation. Word spread quickly around the office that I'd successfully stood up to Bill.

Before Bill left the office that same day, he came by to see me. When I saw him at my door, I was quick to comment, "Oh. Hello, Bill. I suppose you have calmed down now. What is it that you want?"

We spoke about something other than what we'd argued about earlier. Bill's tone was measured.

I knew I couldn't let his earlier behavior go unaddressed, so I ended our exchange by being as clear as I could about my intentions going forward: "Bill, I understand that you were Amrik's right-hand person and now you have become the president. But he is gone. And I am the CEO, the one ultimately in charge of this company. I have to protect the company, and I have to protect the people in it."

When I finally stepped out of the office, Vanessa was still sitting at her desk.

"I have to say," she started, "I always knew you as the smiling wife, happy to chitchat, comfortable being at your husband's side."

I smiled and raised my eyebrows, unsure of what might follow.

"When you took over as CEO, I thought to myself, *This woman has no clue. We are going to have a good laugh when she sees what she's gotten herself into.*"

I appreciated that it wasn't in Vanessa's nature to apologize for thinking such things.

"But you're not a quiet little wife, Ladeira. You're a little tyrant! If there's an issue, you are going to take care of it!"

Overall, I took her words as a compliment. In the short while I'd been CEO, I'd come to understand that Amrik had responded to people's fear or dislike of Bill by finding ways to pacify them or by encouraging them to overlook Bill's bad behavior. But that wasn't going to be my approach.

Later that same week, I overheard our head of sales, Mark, comment to another employee: "You can mess with Ladeira herself, but don't mess with the company. That's when she'll fight you." As I listened, I remembered a night not long before Amrik died, when the security alarm went off in our family home as we slept. Amrik, always the one to avoid conflict, had shaken me awake. "Ladeira. Do you think there's someone in the house?" I rolled over, got out of bed, and made my way down the hall in the dark. By the time I got to the head of the staircase, Amrik had come up behind me and placed his hand on my shoulder. But it was me who started plodding down the stairs to see what had triggered the alarm. In the end, the disturbance had been nothing but an accidental activation of the alarm—likely by a critter passing by.

I giggled at the memory, especially of what I saw when I turned to look at Amrik and Naveen from the bottom of the stairs—the two of them clinging to the wall, their eyes wide. In that moment, I'd been overcome by the sheer silliness of the idea that we might actually defend ourselves against an intruder in that moment.

Sometimes, I felt similarly about my responsibility to protect the company. In my new position, I felt like a woman in her nightgown, creeping down the stairwell, wondering how she would respond to an intruder if one were to appear. Or perhaps more apt, I felt like a bullfighter thrown into the ring without any training but required to hold out the red cape and wave it around, not knowing how the hell I was managing to stay alive for even a second.

During that same early period, five different disgruntled

former employees (all of whom had been let go before I started) also chose to sue the company. To my knowledge, the lawsuits got their start when one of the five—the most recently fired of the lot—contacted others who'd been let go, encouraging them to initiate their own lawsuits. That initial plaintiff was the brother of one of Amrik's good friends from university. Amrik had hired the fellow as part of the marketing team, then terminated him for clearly not fulfilling his job responsibilities. This former employee filed a wrongful termination suit, and like clockwork, there were four more—all of them from people who had been terminated long before Amrik died. I couldn't help but wonder if they all filed suit within the same time frame on the assumption that I would be too ignorant, too fearful, too weak, or too distracted to defend the company against them. I'm sure they believed they could make easy money from a quick settlement process.

Unbeknownst to the plaintiffs, Amrik, to his credit, kept copious and detailed documentation of email exchanges and all conversations leading up to any terminations he instituted. I didn't have to spend much time familiarizing myself with the allegations and then with Amrik's notes to feel convinced that not one of the five suits had legs. If anything, I felt offended by their contentions, energized by their stupidity. There was no way I would back down from the possibility of conflict. I would show up in court if it was necessary, and I would easily defend both Amrik's decisions and the way he chose to carry them out. I made my position clear to the plaintiffs and the company as a whole.

I sent a company-wide notice indicating both my belief that these lawsuits were completely without merit and my commitment to being present in court to fight them. The legal system moves slowly, but when a hearing for the first of the suits finally rolled around, I made sure to attend. Our company lawyer had done excellent work, but I felt I needed to have a voice

in the proceedings. When it was appropriate, I took the opportunity to say, "I will fight to the end to ensure that nobody gets
money they don't deserve." I was sure to look Amrik's accuser
in the eye: "Mark my words, Ladeira Poonian is not going to
pay you a penny." I was thoroughly ready for every one of those
fights, but a short time after the hearing, the first lawsuit was
dropped—the lawyer no longer agreed to represent the plaintiff, because the plaintiff didn't have a case—and the other four
dropped soon thereafter.

Back at the office, Bill had essentially stopped talking to
me. He would often storm out of my office on the occasions
when I called for him, but I was glad that he had decided not to
disrespect me directly.

My next direct confrontations with Bill focused on his
long-standing practice of spending time with his mistress
while on trips to visit with customers. I informed him that
the company was no longer paying for trips that involved this
"perk," and then I did what I could to reduce the overall number of business trips Bill was required to take. To better track
his antics, I made the official decision to take on responsibility
for signing all company checks over a certain minimum mon-
etary amount.

When Bill used his company credit card to pay the bill for
his daughter's emergency room visit, Vanessa once again left
the paperwork sitting noticeably on my desk. For me, this infraction was the last straw. More times than I could count, I
had explicitly informed him that company funds were not to
be used for his personal endeavors. Convinced that Bill must
go but also worried that he might either ignore me or retaliate
if I attempted to fire him, I called on the VCs for assistance.
And in a rare moment of usefulness, they agreed to take care
of it—to have that difficult conversation during which Bill
would officially be let go.

I didn't step out of my office until Bill cleared out his space and exited the building for good. But while I waited, I did manage to overhear a hallway conversation in which someone said, "Ladeira has got some balls!"

I was relieved to see that the atmosphere in the office shifted after that. It was as if everyone had exhaled in unison. If I'd sensed prior to that moment that there were some people sticking around long enough to see what would happen with the company or until they could find better and steadier work elsewhere, after Bill's departure I felt there was a renewed sense of trust among people at the office. My decision was the first big sign to everyone that I was serious about addressing employee morale and ensuring that people felt the office was a safe and fair environment.

With those matters out of the way, it finally came time to deal with the VCs' demands for loan reimbursement.

At the time that Amrik made a loan agreement with his funders, he owned two office buildings. One of those buildings he'd purchased after the business received its first big contract with McDonnell Douglas. Then, as the company grew and needed more space, Amrik invested in another building, which he had used as collateral for the loan.

As it turned out, that second building—our current office space—was worth $2 million. The office building, plus the $4 million the VCs received from Amrik's life insurance payout, ended up being just enough to convince them to accept as payment in full for the $6 million they demanded. I suppose I should have been thankful not only that they had placed a person of their choosing within the company who could give them inside information, but also that one of the VCs had a close personal relationship with our company's banker. When the banker confirmed that there were no other funds they could possibly take from us, the VCs agreed to accept the combination of insurance payout and building ownership.

In response to our new circumstances, we decided to lease

our office space back from the VCs so that we wouldn't have to face the prospect—or the expense—of moving. For the time being, they would leave us alone.

I say "for the time being" because they continued to hold warrants for 30 percent of the company's overall value. They'd already doubled their original $3 million investment, but if the company sold within the decade, the VCs could still lay claim to additional profit.

With the VCs placated for the time being, I could focus on other priorities. As we approached Y2K, our marketing team suggested that we change the name of the software from ShopFloor 2000 to Solumina. There would be no glitches when the clocks switched over into the new century, but the updated product name helped put emphasis on its best feature: the illumination of complex production processes. At the same time that we changed the name of the software, and to make clearer our overall purpose, we also changed the name of the company to iBase-t (short for intelligence-based technology).

We completed the deal with the VCs on a Friday in the fall of 1999. The following Monday, we received our first significant purchase order for that year—one big enough to propel the business forward for an extended period of time. I couldn't help but think that Amrik was doing an angel's work, helping us through this tense and tenuous moment by allowing the VCs to see that we had no money in the bank, then ensuring three days later that we did.

CHAPTER 11

With Bill dismissed and the deal with the VCs completed, I felt the need to make some personnel shifts within the company. Several people started vying for new titles—most of which I changed as requested. I couldn't offer raises to go with all those title promotions, but I sensed that if I didn't improve people's lot, even in this symbolic way, they might not stick with us through whatever challenges were sure to come next. For all the people who wanted their titles changed, I was surprised that only Nick—who'd been a great help to me during the period of working out the deal with the VCs—asked to be appointed president of the operation.

"Give me a try, Ladeira," Nick proposed. "You will not regret it."

Nick had said similar words to the VCs during my first weeks at the office: "Why don't you just give her a try?"

Before he died, Amrik had let me know Nick was someone who *could* be trusted. And Nick had taken the time to teach me what I needed to know to track the company's funds. As I saw it, being trustworthy and loyal to the company put him heads above any potential competitors. I made him president at the end of 1999 with the caveat: "Let's see what you do in this role for a year, and then we'll reassess."

Nick did all right that first year, especially when it came to helping put out fires and monitoring the company's vital signs. So I made his title permanent. In the two years that followed, there were ongoing threats to the company's ability to survive. First, we were affected by the bursting of the dot-com bubble. I wasn't at all eager to reengage with private equity firms, but the general loss of investment funds being funneled into new software companies meant that any additional possibilities for investment in Solumina—or any of its competitors, for that matter—had essentially dried up. Tech companies across the board had become a credit risk. Although I was happy that we were not beholden to investors during this period, I was also keenly aware that we had no investment backing whatsoever—no backstop—should we need to call on funds beyond our monthly or quarterly income.

Back in that first year on the job, I'd learned there was already a consistent hesitancy among potential buyers of our software product, given that it was such a new idea at the time. As a result, the sales team had to put quite a bit of effort into educating clients about our value proposition and offering proof-of-concept contracts so that the software could be tested within the particular manufacturing environments of potential clients before they made a purchase. Those who were interested in Solumina wanted to see if the software delivered the promised efficiencies and production process savings. Although we had a few contracts with big aerospace companies at that point, we were still very much in the process of earning credibility on the market. On top of that, a sales cycle could easily last between nine and eighteen months—all just to lock in a single client. That's a long period of time spent working against people's resistance or reluctance to change. Coupled with investor hesitancy during this same period, we often found ourselves with fingers crossed, hoping we'd be able to make payroll any given month.

The optics of having a former obstetrics nurse at the helm of a high-tech and mission-critical software company did not help move us forward. As they tried to woo new business, the members of our sales team were regularly required to dispel rumors that the company was about to go under. That bit of gossip hadn't confined itself to industry players. I remember Nick coming back to the office from a golf game with a group that included a neighborhood friend of Amrik's and mine. Before Nick was able even to start chatting about his role at the company (a topic he truly loved mentioning), this neighbor steered the conversation to the status of Amrik's company. "Oh, that company won't survive," Nick heard the man say. "Ladeira has no idea what she's doing. It won't be long before we'll see a 'For Sale' sign in her front yard." The group of them agreed heartily.

"What kind of friends do you have, Ladeira?" Nick asked, astonished, after he told me about the conversation.

The VCs didn't make contact with me again until the summer of 2001, this time to let me know they intended to sell the building that we were renting from them as a result of the loan settlement. We needed to move out, which was an expense we hadn't anticipated. Then, in the fall of that same year, as part of the fallout from the September 11 attack on the World Trade Center towers, there was a significant slowdown in aerospace and defense industry investments. Since iBase-t had designed and refined its product in close conjunction with the needs of those two industries, a slowdown in their activity meant a slowdown in ours.

Within months of the September 11 attacks, we reached a major inflection point.

Nick pointed out that we had started hemorrhaging money—about $750,000 each month. "What are we going to

do, Ladeira?" he asked, and my answer was that we had to scale
back significantly.

First, we would have to reduce the size of the sales team.
Amrik, himself an excellent salesman, had invested in a big
team—bigger than any early sales activity would have suggested we needed. Their travel expenses alone were a drain on
the company, as were their high salaries and the fact that some
of them received up-front commissions. We cut the team from
about a dozen professionals down to just two—Mark, the department head, and one of his colleagues. I suppose Mark, who
was a very good salesman himself, had invested in such a large
team so early in the company's existence with the expectation that the software product would be an easy sale. But he'd
been with the company since 1997, and sales hadn't yet been
good at any point along the way. We were selling an industry-
disruptive product and learning that it would take many years
before the market was ready for mass adoption.

Second, I decided to stop taking a salary for a period of
about six months. Next, Nick and I proposed temporary pay
cuts for most of our employees. Nick did a fine job of convincing others to take the cuts—they were still committed to the
well-being and continuation of the company, even during this
topsy-turvy time. But what he didn't do was take a pay cut
himself. Not even a little one.

There was too much else going on for me to pause and reflect on Nick's reasoning for keeping his salary as it was. But
his refusal to make for himself an adjustment he was more
than willing to make for everyone else did call to mind something that had occurred back when we were completing the paperwork to convert his title from its "acting" to official status.
Nick had left a set of papers on my desk for me to sign. When
I looked through them, I noticed he'd written up directives
that would have significantly changed his company privileges.
He'd increased his salary, given himself more stock options,

arranged to convert those options to shares, and given himself the same signatory privileges as me in my absence.

I stepped into Vanessa's office with Nick's papers in hand. "What's all this?"

She had already started making the changes he'd designated.

"Nick already asked me to make those changes." Her eyes opened wide. "Ladeira, I thought you knew!"

I'd walked directly to Nick's office from Vanessa's. Of all the changes he'd made, I felt most insulted by his assumption of signatory privileges, so that's what I focused on.

"Nick, why would I give you the same privileges as me? When Amrik was alive, he designated me to sign for him *only* in cases of emergency. And I am his *wife*! Why would I let *you* sign for me?"

"Oh." Nick was nonchalant. "That's why I left the paperwork on your desk—so you could look it over."

At the time, I'd simply not signed the paperwork, ensured that Vanessa didn't follow through on the changes, and moved on to more pressing matters.

The final thing I needed to do to float us through this period of great insecurity was arrange a line of credit with the bank so that we would have access to emergency funds if we needed them. But to arrange for that line of credit, I had to leverage my personal assets, essentially everything that Naveen and I had to our names. That meant I was risking Naveen's schooling, our home, our futures.

I felt I needed to discuss this with Naveen without also triggering in him any sense of worry. I sat him down by the fireplace in our living room and tried to control my gestures and my voice so that he wouldn't notice that the very idea of risking everything we had went against every fiber of my being. I explained that Amrik's death had changed our lives in ways we couldn't have anticipated and added, "Naveen, you and I only have each other. And we are going to have to look after one another, because we have to make this work."

"Okay, I guess?" was Naveen's initial response. And then, "Mom, I'm seventeen years old! I don't know what to say about your decision. I'm just working on going to school, playing tennis, and having friends." He was right, but the reality of gambling with our little nest egg and his inheritance meant I needed him to know what I was doing, at the very least to acknowledge the risk along with me.

I should have expected Naveen to react as he did. First, I'd protected him from much of the stress and distress I experienced at the company. Second, hadn't he been the one encouraging me—us—to pick up and move forward, just days after Amrik died? I remembered visiting his school to get a read on how they thought he was doing in the weeks and months after Amrik's passing. I hadn't noticed much of a difference in him at home and wondered if he was putting up a front when he was around me but acting out or doing poorly in his classes.

When I went to meet with his high school counselors, it turned out they had the same question for me as I had for them. Naveen was doing so well, he seemed so *normal*, that they wondered if he was having any trouble when he was at home with me! I was getting the impression that Naveen wanted to ensure that everyone thought he was fine. But that wasn't going to stop me from investigating further.

Given the seriousness with which Naveen took most of his courses and extracurricular activities, and given that he wouldn't respond to me directly when I asked how they were coming along, I started sneaking around to observe him and see whether he was, indeed, doing all right. Knowing that he was a very determined young tennis player, I especially wouldn't let him know when I was present to witness his matches. Instead, I would sneak onto school property, unacknowledged, and hide behind the bigger trees to watch him play. Each time I visited, what I saw was a young man who really seemed to be quite fine. Of course, I was both relieved and still suspicious.

Amrik had died the year that Naveen started high school. Now here we were, Naveen already in his junior year and still steadily himself. That hadn't stopped me from worrying about him, especially when he would go out in the evenings to parties and stay out later than his curfew. He was good about always calling to check in with me at the assigned times and ask for each thirty-minute extension for curfew, but I let my mind wander. What if he was only seeming to comply with my rules so that he would have more time to get into trouble? Naveen was at a tender age and bereft of his beloved father's guidance. Might staying out past curfew quickly turn into more reckless behaviors? Drinking? Drugs? Frankly, the older he got, the *more* I worried rather than less.

Right after Amrik died, and not knowing if my initial worries about Naveen's well-being were at all justified, I had called on Mohit, who was raising two teenagers of his own at the time. Our two families had been close right up until the day that Amrik died. After we'd moved to the States and had Naveen, our families would gather in each other's homes on alternating holidays, Naveen thoroughly enjoying his time with Mohit and Dina's two daughters. To this day, I can say for certain that Mohit and his family adored both Amrik and Naveen.

At Amrik's funeral, two of my close friends had overheard a conversation among Mohit's family, led by Dina. Almost immediately afterward, my friends conveyed to Zarine their concern that Mohit's family was both unwelcoming of me and untrustworthy. All that Zarine would tell me then—and all that she told me from that point forward—was that she understood I wanted to like Mohit's family, but I should under no circumstances trust them.

To the contrary, I'd persisted in thinking that our two families would stay close, remain comfortably engaged in one another's lives over the long term. And when I purposefully contacted Mohit with my concerns about Naveen's well-being, I wanted someone who knew our little family to share his own insights about raising teenagers through this challenging period. Mohit's response had been brief and icy: "What do you expect *me* to do about it, Ladeira?" I hadn't asked for Mohit to *do* anything except listen and let me know if he could relate or had any stories to share about his daughters that might translate into useful advice, to allay—or at least help me prioritize—my worries.

In all honesty, that hadn't been the only bit of surprising behavior on Mohit's part. Not long after that strange phone call, Mohit visited us for the reading of Amrik's will and the distribution of his assets. Amrik's family was a rather traditional Indian family, and Mohit, as the eldest son, had anticipated that Amrik would leave everything to him. The tradition that Mohit intended to uphold would require me to ask him for an allowance of Amrik's money whenever I needed it. That would mean asking Mohit for the money to support Naveen's private school education, the money to supply our necessities each month, the money to continue paying our mortgage. According to Mohit's expectations, any asset of Amrik's would be Mohit's to control—including the business—and it would be entirely up to him what Naveen and I were and were not able to afford, what we could and could not do.

When the lawyer clarified that Amrik had left everything to me, Mohit was unable to keep his disdain for me from bubbling over. During our meeting with the lawyer and then after, when we were back at the house, Mohit tried his best to manipulate me into turning responsibility for my and Naveen's inheritance over to him. "Don't you care about your husband's legacy?" he inquired, as if he were clearly the better custodian of that legacy than me.

"You know, Mohit, I wasn't born in India as you were. And in my culture, what's mine is mine. Amrik left everything to me. It's really that simple."

During what remained of that visit and afterward, Mohit found what opportunities he could to be cruel. When I shared with him how the VCs were threatening the company and our very livelihoods, he announced, "I admire them!" When he accompanied me to company headquarters and saw my name on Amrik's office door, he fumed, "It burns me to see your name there." Then, only a bit later, Mohit insisted that I use the money from Amrik's personal life insurance to make an immediate and very large donation to UC Riverside to support an endowed faculty chair in computer science in Amrik's name.

The chair had been set up in Amrik's honor by his former primary investor, the head of the VC group that had caused me such distress. Mohit wasn't satisfied when I agreed to make a significant contribution with the caveat that I would do so *when the time is right*. He wanted so badly for the inheritance to be in anyone's hands but my own. In my mind, and given the daily and weekly crises I was facing at Amrik's company, there was no way I could afford to part with such a large sum at that time. So far as I was concerned, Naveen and I were indefinitely "this close" to losing everything and being thrown out on the street—an assessment even my neighbors had confirmed. Mohit chastised me for refusing to fund the endowed chair right away: "Ladeira, you are greedy, greedy, greedy!" Naveen decided this would make a good refrain each time I denied him some large purchase or significant sum of money to spend with his high school friends. "Ladeira, you are greedy, *greedy, gree-dy!*" he would tell me, a smile widening across his face with each emphatic repetition.

Gradually, I found myself more and more isolated from both family and friends. It was futile to talk with my own family members about the business challenges I was facing—our lives were just so different. I talked mostly with Zarine and Hana. Hana would quickly shy away from difficult topics. "Ladeira," she'd say, "just hearing about what you are facing makes my whole body shiver in distress!" It didn't help that when Phillip returned to Trinidad after his initial visit to California, he told the rest of my siblings that I was under a lot of stress and that they shouldn't connect with me for a while. He meant well by trying to encourage the family not to bother me with any of their troubles, but the result was that I didn't hear from them for quite some time during the most difficult months of my life. If there was anyone I would have wanted to talk to, it was my mother, but she'd begun to decline from dementia and wasn't able to communicate with me as she had during the time before Amrik, Naveen, and I moved to California. We hadn't even told her about Amrik's death, because we knew she wouldn't have understood.

My father had retired when he was about sixty years old. He was thoroughly self-entertaining in retirement—enjoying going to the market and talking with my mother and other family members. He was seventy-nine going on eighty when he fell and hit his head on the bathtub. His brain bled, sending blood into his sinuses, and he died almost immediately.

My mother, by contrast, worked as long as she could, until the point she could no longer physically and mentally deal with it. After she turned the pub over to Phillip, she opened up a little parlor where she sold hand food—candies, snacks, and fruits. When she eventually stopped that business, she also stopped being mentally stimulated. That was when her dementia set in.

I often wonder about the coincidence of those two circumstances. Maybe my mother should never have given up work.

As our mom deteriorated, Phillip's wife, Dolores, was more and more responsible for her care, and less and less interested in being good to our mother. Those two had never gotten along, and my mother's declining health and growing neediness only exacerbated the bad feelings between them. Though Dolores's family had plenty of money, she herself had a penchant for taking whatever she wanted. At some point, she'd decided that she wanted to own the pub and the flat above it, and she did what she could to take possession of those at my mother's expense. I remember my family members telling me that Dolores was putting effort into making my mother forget her family. Dolores would turn over my mother's pictures of all of us children, and in their place, put up pictures of all her family.

Thankfully, my brother Russell—who'd become a Pentecostal priest and ran an orphanage—also looked in on our mother. I would send him money to ensure that she got all her meals and that she was bathed and cared for. With his help, she lived into her nineties, though by then she had stopped recognizing me and would tell me, when I visited, that I looked just like her daughter.

Thinking that I might find in friendships the solace I longed for from family, I reached out to a handful of people with whom I felt connected. Occasionally, I was met with startling responses. When I called on Amrik's good friend from Texas, eager to have someone close-as-family to talk to, he met my initial hello with the unsolicited response, "Ladeira, you know I don't have any money."

I thought about Nick's question: "What kind of friends do you have, Ladeira?"

The thing is, I *did* have good friends and loving family members who stuck with me through dark times.

Zarine continued to visit me and Naveen for four to six weeks at a time, which was my only opportunity to do anything like "entertain" at the house. Quite frankly, Zarine was the one doing the work of entertaining. I'd come downstairs in the morning, and she'd have breakfast nicely laid out on the table. I'd come home from work, and dinner would be served. We'd sit together beside the pool in the evenings and go shopping on the weekends. When she wasn't around, I socialized with Lola and Felix. Lola and I have always had an easy friendship, the kind that comes naturally when you share similar cultural habits. If with some people visits need to be planned and scheduled, with Lola I can do what we West Indies folks do—call from the car when in the area and say, "I'll stop over with sandwiches, and we'll have lunch."

I'd also get coffee or lunch with the moms of Naveen's closest tennis-team friends, or with Sally, the friend whose kind gesture enabled me to acquire an office-appropriate wardrobe. I'm not someone who easily shares the goings-on in her private life, and I had no intention of burdening friends with my problems. When it came to the mothers of most of Naveen's school friends, I was especially careful not to share any distress, knowing that it was possible, even if by accident, that Naveen could learn of some detail I had shared and then worry himself about our well-being.

Beyond visits with those friends, I stopped being social, especially when it came to accepting invitations to parties. Being around other couples at large events was consistently a struggle for me. If I were to attend a gathering, I had to feel that it was important for me to be there—a child's milestone birthday, a wedding, or some other occasion where it would seem rude if I didn't join in the celebration.

I've said I'm not the type of person to open up about my personal life to just anyone. But there were—and still are—friends with whom I've felt I could do that if I needed to. My friends Sitara and Supriya were always inviting me to join them on outings, even when it was my habit to cancel on them at the last minute. And my dear friend Janey, by whom

I felt most understood in terms of her sensitivity to my loss of Amrik, spent countless hours playing tennis with me, going on walks, picking fresh fruit from the garden, enjoying the sunshine, and talking about anything and everything. Although she and I mostly talked about things other than my grief, our friendship helped me work through that grief—or better, live with it. She understood my sadness and seemed to do exactly what was necessary to help draw me out of it enough to enjoy life's little pleasures.

It took quite some time before Anjali and Jatin—the good friends who were so very close to Amrik and who had been such supports to me and Naveen in the hours and days after Amrik died—came back into my life, but eventually Anjali was able to spend time with us without feeling distress about Amrik not being there.

They'd been our friends since we moved from Houston to California and rented a home right next door to theirs. At the time, the couple had recently married, had a child, and moved to the US; it was clear that Anjali was looking for ways to feel more at home with her new circumstances and in a thoroughly foreign place. She had grown up in India, close to where Amrik had grown up, and so she immediately related to him as family.

The four of us grew close quickly. Anjali was always making tea or cooking meals for all of us to eat together. There was a short wall between our yards, and she would climb over the wall anytime she saw me outside. I wasn't as social as Amrik, and my initial reaction to Anjali's enthusiasm was to feel a little nervous about her stepping into our yard. I suppose her natural friendliness triggered my inclination to feel suspicion and proceed with caution. Just as when Amrik had been eager to know me, I'd find myself wondering about Anjali, "What does she want from me?" Before I got comfortable with our friendship, I had to analyze the situation, figure out why she might be interested in my attention, then decide whether to extend my boundaries to invite her in.

When it comes to Anjali and Jatin, I have always been glad that I let my guardrails down. Even after Amrik, Naveen, and I moved out of that home, our family still lived in the same neighborhood as theirs and continued to visit with them quite a lot. We went on vacations together, carpooled to and from school, and their two children and Naveen spent a lot of time playing together.

It was tough for me to lose touch with them following Amrik's death, but reconnecting and discovering that we were so genuinely glad to spend time with one another was a blessing.

Then, of course, there is Sushma; her husband, Neel; and her family, especially her son, Jai, all of whom were then, and have always been, exceptions to any of my rules or feelings about being social after Amrik died.

Amrik had reconnected with Sushma one weekend back when I was still working at the hospital. He had taken Naveen to a service at the local Sikh temple and had made an offering to the general fund while there. It was habit at the temple to call out the names of those who'd donated, and when Sushma heard Amrik's name acknowledged, she decided to see if she could locate him when the service was through. When she had been just a girl, Sushma's parents had taken in a young man named Amrik Poonian during a period of his schooling in India, and Sushma had remembered that young boy as part of her family. Amrik certainly looked quite different in California than he had in India—not only because he was much older but because he no longer wore a turban and had a clean-shaven face instead of a beard. Sushma managed to identify him even with these obstacles in place. She approached him and Naveen, asked about his relation to her family, and discovered that they were, in fact, connected just as she'd thought. Later on, when eventually Amrik learned that Sushma was struggling to find steady work, he offered her a position at his new company. Before long, her son, Jai, earned himself a position in IT, and they both had been working there for three years by the time Amrik died.

That entire family has been like a team of guardian angels for me and Naveen. Whatever happens, there they are, offering concern and care. I have to say, I find it difficult to explain the extent of their generosity as a family. If Sushma were to overhear me saying that I needed to go to the grocery store, I'd get home that evening to find on my doorstep enough food for me to enjoy for at least a week. Neel makes regular trips to India, and no matter what, before he leaves he will inevitably cook me some meat. It's as if he feels badly that he will be away and wants to ensure that I have a suitable protein supply in his absence.

If Sushma notices that I am late to the office or having a rough day, she will check to be sure that I am okay. Once, in the early days after Amrik's passing and after staying late at work, I stepped out to the parking lot and noticed Sushma sitting in her car. When I approached the window to ask, "What are you doing here? You were supposed to leave hours ago!" her frank reply was "You know, Ladeira, you didn't look very happy to me today. I was worried about you, and I wanted to make sure you were okay to drive home before I left." Sushma, Neel, Jai—each one of them sees my and Naveen's well-being as directly tied up with theirs. I see that as part of their generosity, broadly speaking, of the roles they play in whatever communities they're part of. They throw abundant events at their home, and they are constantly at work in their neighborhood and larger community supporting social services—generosity is the very core of their being.

How lucky I've felt to be a member of their community.

From the moment Jai showed up in the days after Amrik's

death to teach me the basics of computers and email, to the many times when Sushma quietly offered me key information about employee goings-on and morale, to all the times they brought me food that would last a whole week or medicines to help me through a sinus infection, that family has proved to be *my* family, through and through. I think of Sushma as a sister and Jai as a second son. I can honestly say that without them, I don't know where Naveen and I would be.

CHAPTER 12

After talking with Naveen about my plans to leverage our assets to support the company, I arranged the line of credit. As it turned out, the business didn't need to access it that year. Looking back on it now, I can say that we survived that year and those that followed for two big reasons: one, we continued to provide mission-critical software for our current clients, including the federal government, and two, despite not accumulating many new clients, we had a small revenue stream from recurring software licensing and maintenance fees. In other words, there was always *some* money, even when the timing of money coming in and money going out was uncertain. To this day, our maintenance contracts, along with our federal division contracts, are what keep the overall operation, particularly the commercial division, afloat.

I should also say that amid all the instability, the company's stellar customer service never waned. To me, this fact reflects the excitement of the engineers and other team members about working directly with customers to refine and develop new capabilities within the software. Amrik had started this business by paying close attention to pain points within the complex manufacturing industry, and we were able to sustain the business through its rough patches—and even its deep anxiety-inducing phases—by ensuring that customers trusted us to show up, listen carefully, and deliver exactly what they needed. This strategy could occasionally cause some distress, as when our VP of sales would come back from a pitch having promised capacities that did not yet exist. But even in those instances, there was still enthusiasm—the thrill, I imagine, of a small start-up environment in which everyone feels invested. Mark would tell the engineers, "If we can build in these additional features, I can get us some more licenses," and the team would get right to work.

Building new capabilities into the software helped yield a more bulletproof product as well as one that could serve an ever-widening set of client needs. We grew our new customer base between 2002 and 2005 as a result of this targeted technical work. Given that bit of growth, we were able to expand the sales team from two members and focus on acquiring big customers like Pratt & Whitney, Sikorsky, Gulfstream, and Lockheed Martin. The original focus of the software concept was workflow processes, and during this period and beyond, we were proving ourselves to have mastered the efficient movement and sharing of information to the benefit of our clients.

During the initial period of his presidency, Nick was thoroughly committed to keeping the company from going under. He understood his job as maintaining the status quo, which in a crisis, is itself a considerable challenge. But over time, I learned that although Nick had the ability to spot a problem, he was reluctant to select and move forward with any solutions. In a sense, Nick was more of a decision instigator than a decision maker. He readily showed me what needed fixing, wondered aloud about potential solutions, and then looked at me to decide what should be done. On the one hand, I took that as a sign of respect that I was otherwise rarely granted by anyone else in management. On the other hand, there seemed a clear limit to what Nick could do with his presidency. Granted, we were making big decisions about the fate of the company during this time, but Nick seemed determined to avoid being at all responsible for those decisions.

He excelled at pointing out dilemmas but was stymied by the possibility of making a mistake. Essentially, I felt he wanted to be told what to do—a fine requirement for someone whose job it is to be instructed what to do at every step along the way, less fine for someone whose job is company president.

So long as Nick could be convinced there was no other option, he was able to act decisively. I remember that he would frequently exclaim, "Oh, shit!" just before taking action, as if to confirm for himself the necessity of whatever he was about to do.

For the most part, he thoroughly enjoyed his title and position and took every opportunity available to introduce himself as the company's president. But in a rare moment of acknowledgment of his own limited abilities, he said to me, "I would never in my lifetime have become president of a company, except for here." Even that awareness didn't seem to lead him to rise to the occasion. It also didn't stop him from fretting that people working in other areas of the company were making more money than him. And it really didn't stop him from displaying an odd insensitivity when it came to boasting about or taking advantage of his position.

Two separate occasions still stand out in my mind.

First, when a forest fire approached the area of town where many of our employees lived, several of them came to the office with their families in tow, unsure about where else they should go. Some of their homes were in immediate danger, so I made clear to the group that if they needed to leave their homes, they were without question welcome to come and stay with me and Naveen rather than have to take up lodging in an area hotel. As I finished clarifying the seriousness of my offer to a room full of distressed faces, Nick came sauntering into the room. I had expected him to acknowledge the awfulness of the threat to our employees and help them feel safe and supported. At the very least I had expected him to notice and react to their palpable worry. But instead of meeting the moment, Nick approached the people he didn't recognize to shake their hands and introduce himself. "Hello. I'm Nick, president of iBase-t."

Second, it had become something of a tradition to hold a raffle at our annual office holiday party. We would all participate by putting our names in a hat, but whenever a name from company leadership was picked, we always set that name aside and took that as an opportunity to pick again—to find a winner who wasn't also someone in charge. One year, when Nick's number was called for the grand prize of an Apple Watch, he happily claimed the prize. When I approached him to suggest that he let someone else be chosen as the grand prize winner, he refused: "I'm an employee here just like everyone else, Ladeira."

Funny how that wasn't the case when I asked you to take a salary cut, I thought to myself.

As the company started to find its footing, I became more and more aware of what Nick *wasn't* doing. He hadn't established any financial goals, or even a budget, and he wasn't working with the heads of departments to strategize or imagine the path forward. Honestly, he wasn't even *talking* to the heads of departments, or to any other employees for that matter. The idea that we were a business that might grow was anathema to Nick's approach. For the most part, he sat at his desk, reviewing and monitoring the company's finances.

As we grew incrementally, I found myself struggling to entertain the idea that we might not always have to dig ourselves out of a hole or face down a significant threat. Though I wanted

Nick to consider and plan for company growth, I still felt inclined regularly to remind him of my mother's words: "Always save for a rainy day." To make sure we children understood her precise meaning, my mother would add, "If you make one dollar, you should save fifty cents." Nick's reply grew as predictable as my words of caution: "I know, Ladeira, I know. Always save for a rainy day."

On the day he asked me to grant him part ownership of the company, I recognized that Nick was someone whose trustworthiness I needed to reconsider. It was true, he had been loyal to the company. Amrik had indicated to me that Nick could be trusted, and I'd found that to be mostly true. But Nick displayed a funny combination of the awareness that titles don't make leaders and the desire to take maximum advantage of the benefits that his title and position offered him. That was what I didn't trust.

If there was one thing for which my upbringing had trained me, it was this: When people start to show ulterior motives, I am always ready to activate the hard shell that protects me from ongoing disappointments. I could always find opportunities to think back to my father's sound advice: "You really cannot trust anyone, especially not 100 percent," or to ask myself the question, *Am I going to hang myself by taking this action?*

Amrik trusted Nick quite a lot.

Then I trusted Nick quite a lot.

But Nick had come on the scene when Amrik was already facing a significant amount of stress and experiencing a growing sense that there were people at work he absolutely could not trust. I had come onto the scene with a sense that Nick was perhaps one of the only people that I could trust, and he had mostly proven worthy of my investment in him. Now that I'd spent several years working with him, I felt authorized to take a step I assumed Amrik would not have—much as I continued to appreciate all the work Nick had done to keep the company afloat, I let myself question Nick's rightness for the role I'd given him. But I also remembered that Nick had not been at all prepared for the role I'd given him. He'd only asked me to give him a chance.

Internally, I was finding my footing as well. I took a renewed interest in making clear to the team that moving up in the company was a matter of one's record of performance and nothing else. Prior to then, I'd taken at least some action in this regard. I'd implemented a policy of meeting with each new employee as they entered the company to instill in them the idea that iBase-t did not operate based on favoritism. At the time, I'd been concerned that new employees would assume that kissing up to their direct supervisors and department heads would be a productive and acceptable way to gain ground. I wanted them to know this was something I would not tolerate, and that my policy would be implemented across all divisions. "Your performance will get you where you want to go," I told each of them, "and your managers have agreed to abide by the same rule." I let them know, too, that I was a CEO who got to know her employees' responsibilities and who read all her employees' internal and external reviews. "If there's a review that I don't agree with, I will have a conversation with that client or with your manager and ask their reasons for writing what they did. I believe in the importance of giving a true review, not opinions or personal feelings. Every employee who joins this company is given a fair chance." I did my best to reiterate these points with existing staff whenever the opportunity arose.

In the short while I'd been CEO, I'd done my best to steer clear of industry-wide or other general gatherings of people in the business world, but one of the events I attended in 2004 put me into conversation with a hospital CEO. When I told him about my training in obstetrics and my current position as CEO of a technology company serving the aerospace and defense industries, his eyes widened in amazement: "My good-ness! How is that even possible?"

How many times I'd had that same thought!

But in that moment, the fact that a hospital administrator was the one asking the question helped clarify my perspec-tive and crystallize my answer. "Think of it like this—*you* don't know much of anything about direct patient care, let alone mission-critical patient care. But you successfully run an en-tire hospital!"

I could see the scowl coming to take the place of his friendly smile, but my epiphany was not going to be slowed by his response.

"You know as well as I do that common sense has a lot to do with being successful in these roles."

Our conversation may have ended shortly thereafter, but I was buoyed by the realization that common sense had been a most valuable resource for me.

My mother didn't have a high school degree, but she had an absolute wealth of common sense that made her one of the brightest businesswomen I knew. Trained in my mother's pub as a young girl and then trained as a nurse who specialized in high-risk pregnancies, I well understood the value of common sense, especially in moments when no amount of specialized training could substitute for quick analysis and decisive action. I'd also come to appreciate the difference between a business crisis and a health-care crisis. In the latter, there was no time to waste. If a patient was bleeding out, I couldn't solicit other opinions or suggest, "Why don't we wait and see what hap-pens." I may have entered Amrik's business at a point of crisis, but the fact that there was time—not an indefinite amount, but always enough to think before acting—made everything a lot easier than I'd imagined it might be.

After chatting with other CEOs, I realized that Amrik and I had taken such different approaches to running the company.

Amrik gave his department heads the ability to do whatever they felt was needed, and he tended to believe what people told him. The result was individuals and departments generally doing their own thing—separate silos functioning well enough without strong communication between them and without a sense of how each related to the other and contributed to the overall project. Making my rounds to talk with everyone and learn what they did had been my way of making sense of that disjointedness, of getting my bearings within the overall scene. It was also my way of assessing what ultimately made sense and what didn't. What I learned was that people were essentially doing whatever they wanted. And that had led to everything from lackadaisical attitudes to abuse and corruption. I could see why having me around and in charge must have seemed like a big shift, and for some, a big intrusion into a scenario with which they'd grown all too comfortable.

A central aspect of my personality—that I don't start by trusting and tend not to believe a word said to me until it's factually proved to be the case—was turning out to be critical to the survival of Amrik's company. But because I'd been a nurse, and a sweet and quiet wife, a lot of people had underestimated my ability. *I* had underestimated my own ability to helm that company.

And I had underestimated Naveen.

Naveen's extraordinary ability to cope with the loss of his father made it possible for me to tend to the company—to learn the contours of its crisis and do what I could to keep Amrik's legacy alive. Naveen's strength, his unwavering realism and his own capacity to move forward with life even in its darkest moments, helped me find *my* strength. My son had a good, solid foundation—principles, scruples, manners, a good demeanor, all the fundamentals of a good person—most of which he learned from his father and me well before Amrik died. But even after Amrik's passing and as he grew into a man, Naveen gathered a good group of friends around him and kept his good head firmly on his shoulders. Because of all that's good in Naveen, I could do what he asked of me that morning when he came into my room, telling me to get up and get to the office because I had a business to save.

CHAPTER 13

If there's one thing that continued to be true since my first day at the office after Amrik's death, it is that no one would willingly park their cars anywhere near mine—certainly not in the spots to either side of me, but also, if they could help it, not in front of or behind me either. Long before I started working there, Amrik had set the scene for people's suspicion of my driving ability by sharing the story of an accident I got into on the heels of a family trip to Australia. I'm near certain he circulated throughout the office, telling everyone about the $13,000 in damages to our car—and a nearby fence—all just from my swerving to avoid a stone in the road. I'm also well aware that just the way I park a car makes people assume it would be dangerous to place their vehicles in the vicinity of mine. I suppose I can understand that. On occasions when I haven't parked quite within the lines, I certainly don't back up and try again. To compensate for my parking habits, the employees developed a policy of leaving the spaces around mine empty until after I arrived, when they could more accurately assess whether I'd parked well enough for them to take a chance on bringing their own vehicles into proximity with mine.

That general perception of my driving ability extended to the people in our neighborhood, and even to some of Naveen's high school friends. Those in the former group were aware of my struggles with any lines demarcating a parking spot, and those in the latter group, well, they liked to tease me about that incident after the Australia vacation, even though it was an event that took place all the way back in 1990.

Naveen was still a young boy then, and at the time, Amrik was working in sales at a telecommunications company called Digital. He was in the early stages of developing a business plan that would enable him to run his own telecommunications company and work for himself, and one afternoon, he'd carelessly left some of that paperwork by the copy machine at the Digital office.

Amrik was a talented salesman. Both at Digital and at the Indian-owned company where he was employed when we first moved to California, Amrik managed to earn the ire of his sales colleagues for succeeding where they did not. It was one of those colleagues and competitors at Digital who found Amrik's business-planning papers by the copier and then decided that the appropriate response was to report Amrik to the boss. The boss didn't ask any questions. Instead, he surmised that Amrik must be running a side business from out of the Digital offices. He fired Amrik immediately.

Our trip to Australia and New Zealand was already on the books when getting fired forced Amrik to get serious about starting his own business. By the time we took the trip, Amrik's recently started telecom operation was teetering at the edge of bankruptcy. We did what we could to reduce the cost of the trip, including staying for some of the time in a hotel that Naveen referred to as a dump. But I thoroughly enjoyed the entire vacation. We got to visit with one of Amrik's good friends from university, and Naveen got to make the acquaintance of a number of sheep, as well as snorkel in the Great Barrier Reef.

Amrik stayed on the boat and refused to get into the water with Naveen when it came time to explore the reef. Amrik had long been uncomfortable in the water, a fact I learned back when he and I took swim lessons together during our time at university. He never learned to swim in India, and I'd never learned to swim at home in Trinidad—the ocean waves there were too substantial and dangerous. The boys would some-times play in area rivers, but we girls were more protected and not allowed to test our skills, even in those waters.

During swim class at the public pool in England, Amrik would essentially drag himself along the length of the pool and occasionally, though warily, push himself across the short side, so long as he was at the shallow end. Even when we built the swimming pool at our house in Coto, Amrik would only oc-casionally jump in, then hold on to the edge with increasing intensity the nearer he got to the deeper water. Naveen was a teenager then, but Amrik would insist on telling him, "You don't go into the pool unless I'm in the pool!" Naveen and I both wondered: *What was he going to do to help?* Amrik liked having a pool, but he truly couldn't swim and remained unin-terested in developing the ability. In Coto, I went so far as to buy a big hook so that I could help him out in case he ever got in trouble in the water.

The day after we returned from our trip to Australia, I'd gone right back to work at the hospital. On the way home, I could feel the jet lag settling in, making my whole body heavy with exhaustion. Close to home, I had started to doze at the wheel when my eyes spotted a relatively small rock in the road. I swerved hard to avoid the rock and ended up taking out about a hundred feet of fence that marked the boundary line of our community. I did quite a lot of damage both to the fence and to my car—I even managed to pop all four tires in the process. From that point forward, people from around the neighborhood would meet me and say, "Oh, you are the one that took all the fence away, right?" From there, it wasn't long before I became the easy object of Naveen's friends' jokes. One of them would always ask, "Did your mom do that?" about any broken fences or other damage spotted around town.

There were other good reasons for people to worry that I might nick their cars or even back into them. I'll admit I could be a little bit dangerous maneuvering in reverse. I'd torn the spoiler off my Nissan Maxima by backing into some object or other. Amrik and Naveen were perennially trying to glue that spoiler back on, but I had a better solution: "We are never again buying another car with a spoiler!" Their chorus of "How about just don't back into things!" never seemed particularly convincing to me.

Just as Amrik was decidedly against improving his swimming, I suppose I was decidedly uninterested in learning to be a better driver, especially when it came to parking within the lines. Call it being focused on other concerns. Call it being comfortable with what I can't do particularly well or with the way things are going, so long as they're going well enough. Call it part of my attitude that we all deserve our fair chances, and then some.

That attitude translated to the approach I'd taken at the office by refusing to consider any employee's termination until that person had been given a full trial of their capabilities. I'd heard from Amrik about all the petty reasons people had been fired from his different work environments. I'd also witnessed Amrik himself get fired from Digital over a misunderstanding. And right when I started working at his company, I'd not done enough to stop an employee termination that I learned after the fact may have been motivated by petty, and discriminatory, assessment.

I'd signed off on the documentation indicating "poor performance" as the reason for termination only later to learn that our then head of marketing may have let go of this employee because his stutter grew more pronounced the more excited or nervous he was. I learned from the little group of people who saw fit to keep me informed about office politics that the head of marketing had more than once shown frustration at this employee's struggle with words, especially when he talked with high-powered clients and partners. I felt deep regret that I'd missed that particular opportunity to work toward a more suitable resolution of the matter. My brother Russell had been a stutterer who became an admired preacher, so I well understood the value of an encouraging environment and some training and therapy. For all these reasons, I wanted to ensure that I didn't let anyone go until all attempts to learn what actually happened and remedy any issues had been taken.

At the same time, I wanted to be sure that problems didn't have time to fester or escalate. When I first became CEO, I witnessed people making very personal decisions involving nothing short of the fate of the entire company. I also noticed that some people were well advanced in the habit of mistreating their coworkers. I wanted to correct rather than perpetuate those behaviors. And I wanted everyone at the office to see that I was not at all afraid to address issues directly and to pull no punches. Instead, we would get immediately to work on any issue before it developed into something more complex and entrenched, or more difficult to address.

I'd taken it as one of my primary tasks to establish a meritocracy where, before I arrived, there had been occasional favoritism and lots of bullying. I needed to prove that rewards were earned by doing good work.

I felt no one challenged me more when it came to achieving these very goals than Nick.

Since 2001, the company had established relationships with some big clients—including United Technologies Corporation, which was a multibillion-dollar organization and conglomerate of companies including Pratt & Whitney, Lockheed

Martin, Sikorsky, and other enterprises. UTC was one of our biggest contracts in the early years of the twenty-first century. In those early years, too, building new functionalities into the software had kept Ted and his team of engineers busy. Ted was his usual critical and combative self, but he was also satisfied with his work. Slowly, our customer base was growing, and everyone was busy ensuring that we were making a success of every client contract we established.

Our customers knew that they could believe in us and invest in our small company even though we were competing against giants in the industry. We listened to them and incorporated what they needed into the product within the time frame they required. UTC had taken the biggest bet on us, and we helped make sure that they saved hundreds of millions of dollars by using Solumina.

It was during this period when we'd achieved steady business—when the flow of money into the company allowed us to sustain it without drawing on the line of credit that I'd established—that Nick wrote himself a bonus.

Actually, he wrote two bonuses—one for him and one for me. He presented them in the usual manner, leaving them on my desk tucked within a pile of other papers for my review. I felt frustrated by this action, as I'd never take a bonus if I couldn't give one to everyone, and I expected him to feel the same way.

Instead of being angry with Nick, I decided that I needed to be even more explicit about my expectations. He'd never been a company president before. I'd never been in charge of a company president before. Perhaps I needed to write out my expectations for the role rather than simply talk with Nick about them.

I drew up a list of things I wanted Nick to do. Some were simple, like step out of his office and talk with the employees; others were more complex, like visit with the customers to let them know they're important, or find out if implementation is going as it should, or see what else the customer might need.

Then I called him into my office. "Nick. You know the employees here are important to me. As are our customers. I've written a list of my expectations for us to review and for you to sign off on, indicating that we have agreed to make these changes." From there, I went over each item in turn—a list of all the things I'd essentially been trying to do myself, all the while hoping that Nick would do some of that work with me. There wasn't much of a conversation between us. I could see that he was reluctant to sign the document, but in the end, he did.

After he left my office, I stepped out into the hallway. Vanessa, whose office was next to mine, called me over to her door.

"You told it like it is, Ladeira! I could hear you in there telling him he needed to pull his socks up and get the work done."

I appreciated Vanessa's confirmation that I'd managed to get my message across. But I wasn't sure that Nick would act on any of the requests I'd made. Frankly, he didn't have to. Not only had I already been doing many of those same things, but I fully intended to continue doing them. And, as before, when I needed someone to discuss pressing issues with, I continued turning to Frederick. Nick officially held the role that made him my right-hand person, but Frederick had fully filled that role. I wasn't about to give him up.

In the end, Frederick was the person I knew I could trust. Frederick was the one who could see all the factors involved in a given situation, help me analyze my options, and then give me the space to consider our conversation and make a final decision on my own. I relished Frederick's input; if anyone was going to give me an unbiased opinion, it was him. And he was always there to help me think when I most needed a thinking partner.

What made Frederick particularly capable of tracing all the contours of an issue and keying in on all the considerations at stake was the fact that people throughout the company had continued turning to him for advice, particularly the team of engineers he oversaw as part of his responsibilities as chief technology officer.

Before Amrik made Frederick CTO, Frederick had begged him not to be put in charge of any people or teams. He didn't want any management responsibilities—not heading up a department and certainly not heading up a whole arm of the business, including product, implementation, tech support, and the like. But Amrik knew that Frederick was a font of knowledge in multiple areas. Frederick had advanced technical prowess and know-how, an ability to think things through to their logical conclusions, and he was well-read and well-informed, always aware of the latest news and analysis on a wide variety of relevant topics. Frederick was our resident genius.

Much as Frederick didn't do things that one might expect managers to do, the other department managers and their direct reports gravitated toward him to discuss technical problems. He was constantly helping people sort things out, willing to engage in detailed conversation when they consulted with him. And they consulted with him regularly.

If Frederick had his own biases, he never showed them— not when he came over to our house for dinner and talked late into the night with Amrik and not when he was under pressure to help ensure that things ran smoothly in Amrik's absence. He may not have been able to clean up his own space—just as he could create a scene of chaos in our house after staying only one night, so too could he make a real disaster zone of his office. Everywhere one looked, there were pens, clips, food scraps, half-drunk bottles of water, piles of paperwork from the side business he ran managing horses—but that man could clear away his prejudices like I'd never seen anyone do.

He was a man of few words, a true confidant and helper, an eccentric, a hoarder, a mad scientist, and someone who was singularly important to the company. Frederick made himself available to me and to people across the organization who might avoid talking to me. Ted, who consistently believed that I didn't deserve to lead the company, listened to Frederick. In my view, that made Frederick an invaluable resource.

I was learning to trust my instincts about people and developing my style as a leader. I would have thought the finances and business development side of the business would be the hardest to learn, but it turned out that the steepest learning curve was around figuring out how people worked and who was truly aligned with and committed to the company's mission.

CHAPTER 14

Buckle down. Fix the holes. Stay focused on customer satis-
faction. This is how we made our way through the first decade of the twenty-first century. We stayed very focused in
our space, even though we hadn't explicitly identified doing
so as any kind of company-wide strategy. Potential clients always had concerns about our size and sometimes about my
leadership—"the accidental CEO" is how I was once introduced to a group of colleagues—but we still had a better product and a higher success rate than our competitors.

As the team was slowly expanding the features and functionalities of the software, I made sure to focus on Naveen's
well-being. That included some additional snooping, this time
on his grades during his first year at the University of Southern
California, or, as it was sometimes called, the University of
Spoiled Children. He'd refused to share his grades with me,
and that led straight to me thinking, *This guy must be flunking
his courses!* It was true that Naveen still hadn't given me any
tangible reason to worry about him, but I continued to do so
anyway.

The one thing that both Amrik and I had been sure to

emphasize to Naveen was the importance of a good education. After Amrik's death, that point took on even greater significance. It became more like a directive: "You *will* get a good education!" I still believed that, when it came down to it, Naveen and I only had each other. I would deal with the company as best I could, but if Naveen was going to get ahead in life, he would have to study and do well in school.

So when Naveen decided that he didn't need me to see his grades, I consulted with Jai, who'd gone to the same school for his undergraduate degree, and who knew how to access the system that allowed students to view their grades online. Jai showed me Naveen's grades—an A+, a B+, and A's in all the rest of his courses.

After a few semesters had passed, I worked my ill-acquired knowledge into casual conversation. "You know, Son, that one B+ you earned your first semester, you know I don't like that."

But Naveen had already gone snooping in my file cabinet—a move motivated by his awareness that I was no longer continuously inquiring about his courses—and discovered that I had printed and kept the records that Jai had helped me access online through the university system.

"And that is why you weren't bugging me about my grades all the while," he announced with such nonchalance that I felt a swell of pride.

Naveen didn't mind that Jai was my secret helper when it came to tracking his grades. He'd grown up around Jai, who was ten years his senior, and that entire family since he was a child. Back when Jai graduated college and applied to work at Amrik's company, Amrik recused himself from the hiring process so that Jai would be assured he'd earned his own way.

I think of Jai as a second son, but Naveen is, of course, my first. Naveen is the person for whom Amrik built his company and for whom I worked to keep it alive.

Before Amrik died, we were already putting him to work

at the company. He started by helping prepare the new office building: pulling wires, getting everything in place to support the large computing systems that were necessary for operation. He was eleven years old and had only worked thirty days when he approached his father for a raise. "I'm working harder than all these other people," he told Amrik, after finishing up a wiring installation. "I really need a raise." Amrik knew the truth of Naveen's claim, and so he gave Naveen a ten-cent raise on the minimum wage he was already being paid. Later on, in high school, Naveen worked at the front desk answering phones and doing odd jobs.

Both Amrik and I assumed that Naveen would be intimately involved in the business—maybe work alongside his dad and then eventually take over. We well knew that to make that transition both possible and seamless, Naveen needed not only a good education but also one that would prepare him to run the business. Majoring in business would ensure that he knew things about running a company that neither Amrik nor I would have learned ourselves.

When it came to the practical application of his more advanced learnings, I made sure Naveen continued to work at the company. During his vacations from college, Naveen would assist the different department managers. He'd complete little projects for the implementation, accounting, IT, and HR teams. Throughout, he understood that he was being given access to each of the departments so that he could get a more complete understanding of how the company functioned—what each arm did and how the different responsibilities and tasks related to one another. Since preparing Naveen to lead was my primary task, I did what I could to add other experiences to his résumé—when possible, shifting him into positions that gave him more responsibility within the various departments.

Back during the months following Amrik's death and as I

learned more and more about the status of the company he'd left to us, I sat down with Naveen for one of our serious talks in front of the fireplace, warmed by that bit of direct heat in a house that otherwise felt newly chilly inside. I can still recall the expression on Naveen's face, at once both wide-eyed and irritated, as I broached the topic of this particular evening's discussion. "You have got to do well at school so you can take care of the company."

"I know, Mom. I know," he'd said, stepping away from the fire and from me.

I know you know, Son. But I need to keep saying it. I'm the one who needs reassurance that we're in this together.

When Naveen was in college, one of his professors invited me to visit the class as a case study of someone who came into a leadership role in a field in which she had no experience. I resisted the invitation for as long as I could, and then, one day, I decided it would be okay to explain to the students how I'd been thrown into an environment in which I had to take control but in which I had no field experience whatsoever. The "hypothetical" scenario that the course professor presented to the class before introducing me was punctuated by the question: "If this happened to you, what would you do?"

I sat in the back of the classroom and got to see how they reacted:

"I'd run!"

"I'd sell the company!"

"I'd hurry up and hire an experienced CEO."

Not until after they expressed their opinions did the professor introduce me, transforming what was for them a funny kind of hypothetical situation—*this could never happen!*—into a concrete example of a scenario worth deeper consideration.

I explained myself to them as best I could: "I had no choice but to try to lead the company. My options were to sink or swim. As you might imagine, I wanted to swim, and so I was going to do everything in my power to make that happen. There were—no, *there are* some important considerations that I keep in mind. My husband gave his life trying to shape this company. I want to honor that. And I want my son to have a good future." I paused before finishing the thought. "And I especially don't want my son to turn to me years from now and say, 'You didn't even make a go of it!' I do what I do because I want to be able to say to him, 'I tried with all my energy and all my heart.'"

I also let the students know there's some truth to the phrase "Ignorance is bliss." Had I known at the very start all that I would have to face in the months and years that followed, I might have thought more seriously about selling the company.

At one point in Naveen's college career, he told me that he wanted to go into investment banking.

O-kaaay, I thought.

I knew he didn't see himself graduating college and immediately working for the company, that he'd imagined a longer, more winding path toward assuming his inheritance, one that gave him experience with other businesses, other responsibilities—one that allowed him to find himself and make his way *elsewhere* than in his father's company. I was willing to see where following his interest in investment banking would take him.

So far as I was concerned, one of the best things that happened next is that Naveen got selected for a banking internship at Smith Barney during his senior year in college. His primary task was to cold-call wealthy investors. To my delight, he absolutely hated it, and by the time he graduated, all he wanted to do was come home for the summer and "take one last summer break" before finding full-time work.

He came home that May, slept in late, swam in the pool, and hung out with his friends.

O-kaaay, I thought again.

His lazing about reached a state of real refinement, one that eventually prompted me to ask him outright, "Naveen, why are you being such a bum?" Then, by late July, all his friends started working at their new jobs, and Naveen's summer of fun came to a screeching halt. That's when he took more seriously the genuine threat of becoming a bum. He was the only one of his friends not working. There was no one left to hang around with. And, thankfully, Naveen was growing bored.

We hired him at iBase-t to work under Nick in an assistant treasurer role. Nick was more than happy to off-load some of his responsibilities to Naveen, but I could tell that Naveen wasn't at all passionate about having a job at the company. He cared about the company, no doubt, but I could sense that the slow pace with which we worked, the unspoken but everywhere-felt goal of breaking even—none of this really excited Naveen. Like everyone else, he came to work, did his job, and went home at the end of the day.

If anything, at that time, it was Frederick who was in a state of permanent excitement, though only in the sense of getting more and more stressed out about his responsibilities. Over the years, he'd grown weary of having the sales team return to the office after most meetings with the demand to add new features to the software so that they could sell more licenses. Nearly every sale had some sort of product commitment tied to it, and Frederick had started pulling out his hair—literally pulling on the hair at the back of his head—in response to the pressure. There was nothing programmatic about their work, no concentrated efforts toward greater efficiency, but Frederick's teams always delivered on time. Occasionally, and to guarantee that they did deliver on time, we had to invest quite a lot of money just to build the newly requested capacity into the software in the first place. But once we did, the team always figured out a way to make it happen. The ability to turn out good product in a timely fashion was critical to our capacity to sustain ourselves in the marketplace. If we didn't offer such careful and on-time customer service and continue to develop our product so that it was essentially customized to each unique business's needs, other companies would swoop in to take our place, and our little business would be dead. If Frederick was under a lot of stress, it was not without good reason.

Even when our teams weren't focused on meeting requests for bespoke functionalities, we were aware of the need to stay on top of new developments in the field. Granted, doing so wasn't always to our immediate advantage. In that first decade or so after Amrik started the business and I took it over, we ended up leaving a lot of money on the table, agreeing to contracts that strongly favored our clients, all because we were a small start-up company desirous of their business. But every couple of years, we'd also launch a new capability and win new blue-chip customers. In 2003, we added maintenance, repair, and overhaul capabilities, and in 2005, supplier quality management and enterprise quality management capabilities. Then, in 2007, Solumina was used for the first paperless power-up on the NASA Space Shuttle *Atlantis*. During the review prior to launch, our software found a nonconformance that allowed the NASA team to lay the shuttle flat and fix the problem quickly enough that they could get it back up without missing the launch window. They saved $15 million simply by staying on track and on time in responding to that single checkpoint in the process.

In 2007, I promoted Naveen from assistant treasurer to treasurer, and everything seemed to be going well enough, but then the economic downturn of 2008 brought us back to that precarious place we'd been in—in my opinion, all too often—in the past. Once again, I suspected we would have to access that line of credit I'd established by staking our home and savings as collateral. For nearly a decade, our personal wealth had been tied up at the bank, a deposit enabling that line of credit. I lived within my means all that while, never imagining that at any point I had more than my salary to rely on. The threat of losing everything had been on the table since 2001, and now here we were again, the business just eking its way from month to month.

This time around, no one had to take salary cuts. Instead, we were able to sustain ourselves by letting go of excess labor within departments. Implementation, sales, product development—we made cuts across the board. For me, it was the first time I'd been forced to take a look across the entire company and ask, in all seriousness, "Who can we do without?" It was a very difficult task, given that I viewed the employees as family.

But the business's survival was at stake.

The year 2008 brought the expiration for warrants held by the VCs. Essentially, holding these warrants allowed the VCs the right to buy or sell shares of the company at a specified price. They might not control the company, but they had cast a shadow over it for a full decade after we reached an agreement about the loans. To my surprise, and as before, back when the VCs *were* in a position to take over the company, they declined. They and their banker friend saw that iBase-t was a company with no contracts coming in, no money in the bank, and essentially no good prospects on the horizon. Instead of exercising the warrants, the VCs allowed them to expire.

And just as before, the very week following the expiration, we got word that another multimillion-dollar contract we were hoping to land had finally come through.

Of course, I attribute that coincidence to Amrik's angelic intervention, as I do yet another transformation that took place that same year.

In the midst of the economic downturn and the layoffs,

and with the threat of the VCs' warrants coming due, Naveen decided to become fully engaged in his work; I could see that he'd become eager to drive better business. The financial crisis had been a wake-up call for him. He'd sat in on meetings, learned about the business, and served as treasurer, but now he wanted to put his business degree to use doing bigger things, like streamlining processes, implementing new ideas, setting goals, and ensuring that we had concrete strategies that could help move the whole company forward. Not only did he see where the company, and where I, needed help, but he was ready to dig in and see what he could do to take the company to the next level.

I knew Naveen had always imagined *that* he'd take over the company someday, but I'd always understood his plan was to work elsewhere for who-knows-what amount of time, then bring his training and experiences back to iBase-t later in his career as a way of postponing *when* he would do so. That approach changed the more he came to see everything at iBase-t that needed fixing.

If Amrik was the angel encouraging synchronicities in the background, a group of senior executives were the angels guiding Naveen within our community.

Back when he graduated from high school and turned eighteen, Naveen decided that he was going to begin his exploration of activities that were now legal for him by taking up cigar smoking. He wasn't a smoker, but cigars carried a certain cachet. They met both of teenage Naveen's criteria for a hobby: they didn't require him to challenge his health and fitness by inhaling carcinogens, and all the big-time CEOs and celebrities were pictured smoking them. So, once he was of age, he took himself to a nearby cigar bar, where he met an established group of successful middle-aged men—many of them CEOs, CFOs, and vice presidents of prominent companies—who were happy to help the new kid learn the ropes. They didn't just teach him how to appreciate cigars; he would also take business questions to them.

In my conversations with Naveen, I'd sometimes suggest, "Naveen, why don't you ask your cigar-bar friends what we should do about this issue." In a sense, Naveen had quite naturally entered a social network that would help him learn his way around complicated issues that CEOs and CFOs dealt with on a regular basis. Regularly showing up to that cigar bar was like showing up to his own personal advisory board meeting of very successful people. In an important sense, they gave him that access to other companies that he so wanted, without him ever having to go work for them. For that alone, I was most grateful.

Naveen had been well received within the company when he came on board as assistant treasurer and then earned promotion to treasurer. When he started getting more involved with overall business strategy, people mostly kept their opinions to themselves—if they even had opinions. The only negative comment I heard about came from one very new, and very young, hire—a fellow right around Naveen's age—who said to him, "As the son of the company, I'm guessing you can get a good position really fast!"

The son of the company. What a funny way of putting it.

All the while I'd been leading Amrik's business, I never once imagined that there would be any negativity about Naveen taking on roles with greater and greater responsibility at iBase-t. He was set to be its beneficiary, for goodness' sake! Why wouldn't I try to make sure that he learned everything he could? Why wouldn't I let him try out different roles to see where his interests and talents would be best put to use?

What sort of mother would I be if I didn't do these things?

CHAPTER 15

When I became CEO of Amrik's company at the end of 1998, I saw just how terrible a predicament it was in.

Over and over again, I thought to myself, *How could my husband leave me this mess?*

I'd kept things afloat for a decade by the time Naveen chose to get more involved in company leadership, ensuring as best I could that the business survived at least until then, that Amrik's vision didn't die with him. I mentioned earlier that I attribute Naveen's attitude shift from disinterested employee to focused leader to Amrik's divine intervention, but also that the 2008 financial crisis and its direct effects on our capacity to do business brought to light for Naveen the precariousness of the company that would become his inheritance. The most serious question for him, I see now, was this: Did he, in fact, *want* to drive forward the legacy of his father's company? Or would he let it plod along, working to make its handful of loyal customers happy, hosing down fires here and there as they inevitably arose?

What Naveen saw when he decided to engage was a

business limping along with little direction or strategy. Little planning. And no vision for growth that we could see.

What Naveen saw was a mess.

His first inclination was to inquire into the real possibilities for growing and expanding the business, rather than merely sustaining it. And the first thing he did to follow up on that inclination was to conduct a market analysis. In this way, he would find out both where we should be selling our product and how we should be selling it.

Despite Naveen's best efforts, and for some time thereafter, the company still had no annual budgets, no revenue forecasts.

Looking back on it now, in all honesty, I don't think I'd spent a day on the job when I or anyone else dared to look ahead to where we could go. We were focused almost entirely on survival.

Moving forward would mean having to get our acts together in ways we had yet to consider, let alone attempt. Moving forward would also create more work—at least for a while, and especially for the department heads. It was time to double down on making sure our employees could work effectively together as a team through what might be a stressful time, something that had concerned me for some time. Mark, still head of sales, appreciated that we needed a strategy. Frederick was eager to see if having more formalized processes might alleviate some of his stress, and Ted—well, Ted continued to wonder why we thought we knew anything about what he and his team might need to do.

For all my efforts to make certain that people were respectful of one another at work and that department heads promoted their employees based on trackable merit, we had never really achieved any sense of being one team coordinating our efforts or working together toward the same stated and agreed-upon goal. Instead, whole teams could still feel as if they were at the mercy of other teams—as when sales would demand a new feature be added to the product for the sake of increasing the numbers of new contracts and software licenses, and the product team would feel pressured, sometimes bullied, into satisfying that demand without discussing options or alternatives.

The time had come to bring in a consultant and get everyone on the same page.

In 2014, we invited Mitchell to offer his executive coaching and training program to the entire management team. He began by talking with us about what was *not* working, arguing that we needed to get everything out on the table before we could find our way forward. When it came time for the airing of grievances and discontents, I have to say, I both understood and was a bit surprised by people's sentiments and the depth of some of their resentments. That first session with Mitchell during which we identified our problem areas was what Naveen tells me is called a bitch fest.

Some issues were obvious: After all this while, we had yet to develop a road map for the future and were just moving from one project or concern to another, finishing putting out one fire while running in the direction of the next. Other issues were less obvious: While everyone felt there was an immense amount of accountability when it came to growing and maintaining our relationships with clients, many felt there was a lot less accountability governing our interactions with one another. People noted that they had very little trust for other employees or other departments, and nearly everyone felt there was no healthy debate about ideas. Instead of working together, each person looked after themselves. They sensed that the company would do just about anything to increase its revenue, no matter how much that also increased pressure on individuals, teams, or the organization as a whole.

It smarted to hear those critiques, to think about their legitimacy. My first day on the job, I'd given myself three areas of focus as CEO: employee well-being and morale; business productivity and efficiency; and providing the tools people needed to succeed. I suppose I had done a fine enough job of the last one; all anyone had to do was explain the need to invest in a helpful device or instrument, and we acquired it for them. But the others? Whew. I'd tried so hard and yet not gotten very far in the long run.

Mitchell was a godsend when it came to helping us through this difficult moment. He offered one-to-one coaching for each member of the executive team in addition to ongoing strategy meetings and group training sessions. Most attended both eagerly or at the very least with some curiosity about what might come of the effort. We made some hires and got to work systematizing our budgets, which had been in an ad hoc state until then.

Jason and Terry were our first executive hires from outside the company, brought in under Mitchell's advisement as vice president of product and vice president of marketing, respectively.

The first thing Jason asked when he got settled into his office was "Where are the budgets?"

Nick and our controller, Edith, had done some work to create a semblance of budgets, but they hadn't gotten very far with that project by the time Jason posed his innocent question. In other words, no budgets had been documented. Instead, there'd been some loosey-goosey budget strategizing conversations with the various teams, after which no one seemed to stick with the plans.

In addition to helping us generate official budget documents, Mitchell gave me and Naveen some perspective on leadership, hiring practices, and other fundamentals necessary for transforming the company. The more I learned from him, the more it seemed to me like a miracle that we'd managed to continue winning and keeping business over the years while other similarly small-company competitors had been gobbled up by billion-dollar companies. I suppose staying focused in our space, keeping industry-trusted experts on our staff, and having excellent customer service had helped us stand out. Now, to keep standing out, we had to look inward. In that moment, our biggest priority was solving problems regarding how we functioned in relationship to one another.

Mitchell challenged me to change my mind about my policy of repeatedly giving people chances to prove themselves. Honestly, unless someone tried to steal from the company or tried to start a coup, I kept them around and looked for positions and departments where they might be a better fit. I'd even gotten into trouble trying to offer last-minute help to an employee to whom I'd given second, third, and fourth chances to succeed.

Things didn't go so well for others, though I still understood them to be exemplary of Mitchell's point. I've noted that people had grown comfortable with the lack of oversight and were taking advantage of the company in ways both big and small. There was one employee, for example, who had incorporated her grocery shopping into her regular workday activity. One afternoon, when I found myself having to run to the local store for a sandwich, there she was with her shopping cart, buying groceries. I thought, *Okay, she's obviously going to take those groceries home and then come back to work.* Back at the office, I asked one of the women at the front desk to let me know when this employee returned to work. Well, she never came back to the office that day. Her supervisor wasn't asking about her absences, and she certainly wasn't offering any updates. *Okay,* I thought, *she must have officially taken the afternoon off work.* But no. When I followed up, I saw that she claimed to have worked a full eight hours that day. When I asked her supervisor, "Did you know that so-and-so was not here all day?" he had no idea that she'd left work and been gone all afternoon.

Only occasionally did discoveries like that one sort themselves out without my having to follow up or take action. But
on one memorable occasion, when I'd taken the day off for my
birthday and gone to the mall to do a bit of shopping, I saw one
of our department heads, waved enthusiastically, and started
walking toward her. But she started running away! Of course,
I ran right behind her, calling out her name and asking, "Hey,
how are you?" She was unwilling to engage me, and within the
week she had submitted her resignation.

Mitchell's coaching helped me see that hard workers,
smart people, and even good people weren't always also good
employees, leaders, or managers. I came to understand that the
executive team needed to be composed of people who knew
how to drive an organization and that we needed to work on
removing people whose effects on the company were harmful
or even toxic.

That was a hard lesson for me. It was one thing to understand Mitchell's point, yet another to implement it. As hard an
exterior as I tried to maintain, my softer side grew sick at the
idea of giving up on people who stood with the company, and
stood by my side, during its most difficult periods. For Naveen,
Mitchell's advice had almost the opposite effect. Since he'd
started at the company after graduating college, Naveen had
been eager to fire everyone, or at least eager to tell me that's
what we needed to do. I'd try to talk him out of his opinions,
or at least talk him down from the adamancy with which he
held them. When Mitchell came in and gave us the confidence
to provide more structure, tighten some people's ropes, and
take a clear-eyed look at what was not working, it was as if he'd
confirmed what Naveen had known since day one and what I'd
coaxed us both into putting out of mind.

When we hired Jason and Terry, we seemed to be on the
right track. Jason, as VP of product, showed us that by building in features and functions every time a customer asked, we

weren't thinking about making a scalable product or about selling the overall value of the product to the market in a broader sense.

Terry, as VP of marketing, helped us think about how we should approach product sales to put more emphasis on market value.

As Naveen started to assemble a new management team, resentments developed among the people who'd been with the company and in their same roles for quite some time. Mark and others decidedly resisted new management. And some of the new hires were rude to the "old blood," treating them as amateurs undeserving of their attention or encouragement.

When Naveen brought on two more people, Larry to serve as vice president of sales and Solomon in the role of chief customer officer, things got even tenser. Mark, who had proved time and again that he was a superior salesman, was not the right person to head a department. Some of the old guard felt thoroughly diminished and thrown aside. After a while, I found myself agreeing with Mark that Larry, his new boss, may not have been the good choice we originally thought he was. I understood both sides of this tricky situation.

For all the new efforts we were making to build stronger relationships, our executive team strategy meetings were growing more intense, with one of them turning into a true shouting match. What I remember of the scene in the conference room during that meeting is Naveen pouring himself a glass of Scotch midday, someone yelling at the top of his lungs, "You don't know shit!" and another member of the group rising up from the table with a grand gesture and walking straight out of the room.

So far, we were the antithesis of a cohesive executive team.

It took time to get it right. There was trial and error. There were hard-won lessons. There were hard decisions along the way. But all the while, we were making real progress. There would have to be other changes to the executive team before we found the right people to get us to the next stage of development. As we worked on hiring, Naveen kept building the infrastructure we needed. To me, it looked like he was reading every leadership and software book ever written! Between gaining greater familiarity with the market and with his leadership responsibilities, and then meeting with Mitchell to continue trying to get the right people into the right positions, Naveen had his hands full. I promoted him to chief operating officer so that he could have a position within the company that would clearly give him the authority he needed to make necessary changes. I'd brought the company to a certain point in its lifespan, but it needed Naveen to take it to the next level. I couldn't have been happier that even through this bumpy transition period, he still found himself wanting to stay.

One of the biggest challenges of my career was sorting out what to do about Nick. I was torn between my intense loyalty to him and my knowledge that there wasn't a place for him in this new structure. It was an agonizing time, as I recalled how much I relied on him in the early days when I took over. It took a long time for me to come to grips with this decision, but I ultimately had to side with the company. We offered Nick an alternate position, and he decided it wasn't a fit. Though it was a difficult moment for me, it was the right outcome.

In the midst of all these shifts, we lost Frederick. He'd been Amrik's dearest friend and my confidant and greatest guide in Amrik's absence. Frederick had gotten so accustomed to being stressed that it had become his singular mood. Eventually, the stress that drove him became the stress that stopped him.

His wife told me that he'd been cranky all morning on the day he died, frustrated with her and showing off his temper. When she brought him breakfast in bed, he was angry—near furious—with what she'd prepared for him. She left the room to clean up the kitchen, thinking he could benefit from some time alone to settle down and maybe even change his mind about breakfast.

When she went back upstairs to check on him, she found him dead, the untouched plate of food sitting squarely on his chest.

Losing one of our most trusted leaders made clear to me that I needed to lean more on Naveen than ever before. Although I had come to accept that change was inevitable, I also realized that Naveen was going to be the person I could count on most.

CHAPTER 16

Shortly after that, I made Naveen president of the company. I was pleased to see that most people at the office both expected and were happy to see Naveen take the lead. By the time it was official, he'd already done so much to shape the company's processes and systems, increase its business and income, and shift us beyond survival mode. Even if there were employees who still wondered if Naveen would be able to move us forward, everyone was unquestionably happy to see Nick leave and knew that, at the barest minimum, Naveen's appointment already marked a significant improvement in the company's circumstances.

I was more than happy to defend Naveen to those who underestimated his talents. But after putting Naveen in charge, I was initially shocked that sharing decision-making power with him turned out to be a real challenge *for me*. He has his ideas. I have my ideas. These often are not the same, and so there's been a good amount of fighting between us. When Nick and some of the others were still around, I had a stronger sense that Naveen and I were working together, jointly identifying problems and generating resolutions. I also believed myself to be very clear when I appointed him: "You can be in charge, Naveen, but I need to know *everything* that goes on." If I was going to consider taking more of a back seat and only getting involved in decisions that related to the overall fate of the company, I needed assurance that Naveen would keep me as informed and engaged as I saw fit.

Thankfully, it's easy enough for the two of us to be aligned when it comes to company culture and most HR matters, as well as our commitment to open-door policies and ongoing conversation and check-ins with employees across the board. We've also continued working together to get the right people into the right roles—a project that has taken some patience and effort, and one that, so far as I can tell, will always feel as if it's ongoing.

But where Naveen and I regularly find ourselves in conflict is over money.

I can still hear my mother's voice instructing us kids, "Always save for a rainy day." Experience has shown me the great benefit of heeding that bit of advice with care. But Naveen? He often wants to spend money in ways that don't make any sense to me. I've said Naveen never does anything without having a good reason, but some things I just have to question. He'll suggest that we take the entire staff on an annual vacation, and I'll counter that perhaps we should just have a nice party. Of course, even when we do have a party, we'll each have different ideas about what qualifies as "nice." I'll suggest that a hearty sandwich spread and some of my homemade soup would make for a friendly gathering. Naveen will want things to be refined and elegant and won't care how much it costs to ensure that's so. Does elegance require a couple of large floral arrangements and some high-top tables? So far as he's concerned, it does. As a result, our heads of HR and administration much prefer turning to him for guidance when it comes time to prepare an event. But here's the thing I can't turn away from: I have gone through two rainy seasons, and it was because I saved for those rainy seasons that we were able to get out of them. Naveen has never gone through that experience, so he is far less convinced about how much money we need to have in the bank in case the weather changes.

When I was in school, every penny counted. I had to support myself living in another country. By contrast, Naveen had an allowance in college. I paid for his school, his books, his lunch, everything. And then I would give him $200 extra a month for whatever else he needed. When he argued with me that he was going to school in Los Angeles and that the cost of living there necessitated a higher allowance, I would think to myself: *How much more money does he want? And what will he use it for?* I had to live within my means, and I think it's an important life skill to have. I argue with Naveen about money, because I want Naveen to understand its value. I keep on telling him money doesn't grow on trees. I remember like it was yesterday the time that I didn't have half a dollar to contribute when the girls came around at work to collect for someone truly in need.

Very recently, we've moved office buildings again, this time returning the company back to the very space in which it got its start. We maintained ownership of the building over all these years, and now that we have more employees than ever working remotely or simply from their homes nearby, we no longer needed to rent as much space as was required only a handful of years ago. When we were planning for the move and for downsizing, Naveen wanted to purchase all new furnishings; he insisted that everything should match, and everything should be brand-new. But I was committed to having my same office furniture, originally Amrik's, transported from one building to the other. Sure, it needed a bit of refinishing and touching up, but it's perfectly good furniture and in no need of being donated or disposed of. Why not continue utilizing what still has some life in it, and save money for other things?

Occasionally, it seems to me that Jai and Naveen share the same attitude about spending money. Jai insists, for example, that I always own the most cutting-edge gadgets. Of all people, he knows I'm not fond of learning new technology, but when I'm not looking, he'll sneak a new device into my bag. "Why did you do that!" I'll ask, every single time. "You know I didn't need anything new!" His argument is usually fairly convincing, at least when he insists that it will reflect poorly on the company, and on him personally as the vice president of IT, if I'm not using the most up-to-date technology whenever I'm out in public. Outmaneuvered, I'll shoot back, "Well, now you're going to have to teach me how to operate this thing."

If I've lived by any rule, it's this: You do what you can with the money you have. To this day, I am committed to not borrowing money from anybody. It's true that one motivation for my approach comes from having had to dig Amrik's company out of a terrible borrowing arrangement. I can still feel in my very being what it was like to have those VCs at my throat. But even if that hadn't happened, I don't believe I'd have taken a different tack. Living within my means was a habit I had long before there was any trouble. And on top of that, I have read about and even seen firsthand companies that fall into the same operating pattern: They borrow money, they spend it quickly, and then, whoops, they go under, or they have no choice but to get scooped up by a bigger and wealthier competitor.

In all honesty, what worries me to this very day is the thought that Naveen will one day see fit to have the company take on debt again.

I believe our company's past offers a stark lesson in the value of not owing anybody anything—and especially not trying to grow a company quickly using loans, or worse, using investments that come with all sorts of strings if not outright limitations. To the contrary, Naveen asserts that the problem is actually smaller in size and significance: His father made a horrible deal, and now, we're a company experiencing different circumstances in a different world. Naveen reasons that one bad deal in the late 1990s doesn't necessarily mean it's a bad idea to consider new lending arrangements.

I suspect that the two of us are bound to see this matter differently forevermore. I don't understand why a company needs to grow quickly, and I'm acutely aware that trying to grow the company quickly was so stressful for Amrik that it shortened his life. He'd been open to borrowing money from whoever offered it, and he'd not hesitated to risk our livelihoods in the process. When Amrik died, he left a company deeply indebted to investors who had no knowledge of the technology he was developing and no interest in seeing the company succeed except to turn a profit. They wanted a return on their investment, period, and they showed me that they'd get it by whatever means necessary.

Then, in the time that followed, not once, but twice, I had to wager all the money Naveen and I had to keep the business afloat. When I think about my upbringing, my time supporting myself in England, and the precariousness in which Amrik's business venture placed us for nearly a quarter of a century, I shouldn't be surprised that, to this day, I'm still far more comfortable making budgetary cuts than I am spending money.

If I'm honest, I suppose I shouldn't be surprised, either, that Naveen's inclinations are quite the opposite of mine. Naveen is exactly the son that Amrik and I raised. Whereas I've felt I had only myself to depend on for much of my life, he's never had the experience of wondering if he has enough money to eat, to pay rent, to sustain himself through a difficult period. At least in that sense, he's always had his father and me there to protect him and ensure things are okay. And I have always been saving so that I could see us through.

What Naveen knows for sure is that there will always be a cushion beneath him should he fall, and there will always be sunshine after the rain passes. What I know for sure is that there will always be a rainy day. I will always have to watch how I spend, at the very least because one can never know for certain what turns the economy will take. Keeping a close eye on the money and avoiding waste will always be a good plan.

I've overheard Naveen describe himself to others as the yin and yang of his mother and father. If his mother is far more interested in saving money than spending it, his father leaned toward excess, enjoying the best in life, even risking insurmountable indebtedness pursuing the belief that his product would forever change the way complicated manufacturing processes worked. Naveen negotiates both inclinations; though, from my point of view, of course, he is his father's son.

And so, we sometimes struggle to lead the company together. Our business disagreements are permeated by the push and pull between mother and son, each with different life experiences informing our opinions and positions. I left Trinidad because I wanted to have a better life and to have options different from the ones I saw around me, and Amrik and I made the choices we did because we wanted our son to have a better life—more options than we had. I don't want Naveen to have to repeat my life experiences, but I *do* want him to understand my reasons and recognize the value of my approach. I wouldn't mind it if, occasionally, he also took my advice.

The closest I get to making that happen and to resolving disagreements between us is to turn to Jai, who's become the go-between for me and Naveen. The way I see it, Jai often succeeds in convincing Naveen when I can't.

When we were planning our move back into the company's original building, besides insisting on keeping Amrik's desk and office furniture, I asked to occupy the office that had been Amrik's when he started the business in the mid-1990s.

To me, it made perfect sense to return his furnishings to their original space and to claim that space for myself. Naveen had already selected another of the offices as his own, so there was no chance of a direct clash between us.

But Naveen saw it otherwise. Amrik's old office is a very nice corner office, and Naveen wanted to offer that space to another of the higher-ups in company leadership as a sort of perk. Naveen even proposed to create another, much nicer office for me.

I explained to Jai the sentimental value of that space. I wanted to be where Amrik had been when it all started. I had helped get us back there, and I had already imagined myself in that space, down to the detail of identifying exactly where I would place Amrik's photo so that I could glance at it easily throughout the day. Jai understood my feelings and intervened on my behalf, explaining to Naveen: "Nobody else should be in that office besides either your mother or you."

Naveen understood and agreed.

Of course, not every negotiation of the family dynamic that lands on Jai's plate is as simple as determining office space. Sometimes, I'll have a more amorphous request, like: "Jai, here's what's going on, and I really need Naveen to be involved. What can you do?" Maybe it's because he's distinguished himself as a problem solver, or maybe it's because he really cares about and wants what's best for the company, but Jai will treat my requests with the same seriousness as he approaches any dilemma in our IT network. He won't just get it fixed; he'll look into the causes of the problem, and he'll follow through to address those as well.

I've told his mom that sometimes I refer to Jai as a second son, and Jai himself teases me: "When you sell the company, let's see if you still feel that way."

The more I think about it, although it may seem like Naveen and I differ most when it comes to our attitudes toward spending and saving, I suppose that's more an expression of the real core of our disagreements, which comes down to matters of trust.

I learned the value of distrust at an early age, but reminders of its value have repeated themselves over and over again throughout the whole of my life. My upbringing in Trinidad certainly provided early training, but my experience leading Amrik's company through a period of personal and business crisis only solidified that training into a protective habit.

My inclination is still to believe no one until there is a significant amount of evidence in favor of trusting them—and even then, I make sure that I don't believe or trust more than the 80 percent my father recommended to me as a reasonable, healthy value. This outlook protected me as a young woman from suitors with less-than-pious intentions and ultimately saved Amrik's business during a long period in which there were multiple opportunities for it to be shuttered. To this very day, I will assert with confidence that there wouldn't still be a business if I hadn't questioned and second-guessed people's motivations and intentions, or if I hadn't approached troubleshooting with a goal of gathering information, analyzing it as thoroughly as I was able, and then deciding for myself—always in that order.

Even Amrik, trusting as he was, when he became an entrepreneur, warned me never to sign anything I hadn't reviewed thoroughly. Even Amrik had warned me never to trust that others would be honest in their business dealings with me.

After Amrik and I married, I'd trusted him implicitly. I signed whatever documents he put in front of me, believing that he was taking care of everything and that I needn't pay attention to the details. What I learned when I took over the business is that I should have been paying more attention— even to him. Had I signed off on documents that contributed to our indebtedness? Had I trusted Amrik too much?

As CEO, I was immediately more careful—reading documents that came across my desk multiple times if that's what seemed necessary to ensure I understood the details.

Except for once, when I let down my guard and assumed that the people working around me were also being vigilant in their review of contracts.

Very early on, there'd been a contract passed back and forth between our sales team and the client. The client made some last-minute changes, and the sales team signed off on them and sent the document to me for final approval. At that time we absolutely couldn't afford to lose any money, and I assumed the team had reviewed the changes carefully with that knowledge. I signed my approval without reviewing the document in full that final time.

We ended up losing about half a million dollars in additional implementation work the client had added to the final document.

I had taken a break from my own cautiousness, counted on others, and contributed to a loss of funds we so desperately needed. I learned my lesson well in that moment. Never again did I simply skim a document or look only at the sections where I knew to expect that revisions had been made. On the chance that even the slightest detail may have changed from one version to the next, I needed to reread every word. By the time Nick started trying to sneak changes to his contract and bonus requests past me, I was already well practiced and ready for careful review.

I've tried to instill in Naveen the same vigilance that has protected me on more occasions than I can recall. But to Naveen, my approach makes no sense. When I suggest that he operate from a place of distrust, he'll ask me, "Mom! How can you live like that, believing in no one?"

I say he's like his father, trusting far more than others

deserve. But it's quite possible he is a bit like me after all, that he was listening to me all those years I followed him around the house attempting to offer him life lessons, then followed him around the office doing the same. After all, though he's still far more trusting than me, he also doesn't trust blindly. If I begin every interaction with the thought *I will not trust you until I see regular evidence that I should do so, and then I will still not trust you entirely*, Naveen begins every interaction with *I trust you, but I will also need to see evidence*. In this small way, I believe, I've had some effect.

It's an effect I'm glad to have had. I'm convinced it's one thing to support people guided by the idea that they might at some point step up and step into the chances they've been given, the space that's been made for them to succeed. But it's entirely another matter to begin with blind faith, or to think it's acceptable to count on someone else, *rely* on them to meet your needs or to live up to the same standards to which you try to hold yourself.

That said, I've occasionally wondered about my commitment to not trusting anyone entirely, because that attitude applies even to my own son.

When I say that I follow my father's advice to never trust anyone more than 80 percent, this applies also to Naveen. I don't take as truth everything that Naveen says to me. I listen, I analyze, I investigate, and I do what I can in response, on the chance that I might someday need to take care of myself.

I was probably around ten or eleven years old when our next-door neighbor came into the pub and lingered at the counter, talking with me about his children. He'd turned his property and his savings over to them, hoping they'd be good stewards of both and that they'd provide for him as he aged. Instead, he'd ended up with nothing. When he asked his children for assistance, they refused, pointing out, "It's our money and our property now." Here was this sad man crying and telling a ten-year-old girl his troubles. He didn't care whom he was talking to, so long as that person would listen.

I listened. And I came away from that exchange thinking how lucky I was to have learned from his mistake. I would always have to protect myself.

As I've aged, I've given Naveen access to some of my financial information, but not all of it.

I love Naveen with all my heart and then some. I've lived this life for him.

But if there's one thing of which I'm certain, it's that I can't say for sure what the future will hold. None of us can.

CHAPTER 17

The technologies that we utilize internally have changed dramatically as part of our efforts to drive more efficient business processes. Every change we make ensures that we continue to offer a product built for the future, one that still honors our customers as we track and respond to their needs. Making use of cloud technology, e-learning, and related digital innovations has taken the friction out of deployment and made product scaling possible. Before, everything we did relied on individual people and tribal knowledge; now, we've translated that knowledge into technology and processes that allow people to deploy our product remotely and use self-help features to leverage the most out of the software. What that means is that we no longer have to travel to faraway places to set up and train clients there.

But we haven't changed so much that we've eliminated in-person attentiveness to our customers. Though some of our employees work from wherever they happen to be located, others still work near and are in direct contact with our biggest customers, every day confirming the ongoing value of personal interactions. And although we've transitioned to a smaller headquarters, and many are enjoying working from home most days, I still really enjoy being part of the office environment. I'll never choose being at home over being in the office and getting to check in on everyone, finding out how their work is coming along and how their families are faring. Those who feel similarly still have an office to go to. Some want their home to be their home, their work to be their work, and the two never to overlap. Others want the opportunity to collaborate and innovate in an offline environment. The ones who are busy bees like me want to be in the office to have a stronger sense of what everyone else is up to.

Our current CFO remains amazed that Naveen and I don't access company money for our own benefit. "You even buy your own meals!" he'll report back to us, incredulous. And for all his desire to spend money on our employees, Naveen has incorporated at least some of my influence, insisting on flying coach, even when his executives travel on the same plane in business or first class.

With Mitchell's continued coaching efforts across departments and his role on our advisory board, we've finally done the work of establishing and sustaining internal business processes, including clarifying the structure for what happens when particular questions or issues arise. Everyone is now aware of how workflows are managed, issues analyzed, and plans executed, and everyone documents their efforts for the sake of learning and improvement. Individuals and teams no longer risk either having no idea what the others are doing or stepping on one another's toes. Clear processes and guidelines keep both employees and customers from avoidable frustrations. Each department has its goals and understands its role in making the company successful.

When I look back on that first set of external hires we made in 2014, I can see both why we hired those particular people and why some ended up not working out. For all the knowledge they brought with them from prior experience and training, some people were clearly more comfortable with their own ego toxicity than with succeeding as a team in their assigned roles. The business smarts they brought to the table— the very qualities that had so much attracted us to them in the first place—didn't matter when it came to the way they treated everyone around them. The name-calling, the yelling, the conviction that their way was the only way—these qualities could not be shifted and ultimately undermined the company's success.

Sometimes, I still cannot help but wonder, *Are there lots of businesses that accept this sort of abrasiveness as normal? Do people pound their fists in meeting rooms everywhere?*

I remember Naveen and I talking with Jason and Larry early on, trying to set things right with each of them to help their teams succeed. So many times, Naveen responded to Jason's rants and outbursts with a clear-enough directive: "If there's something you need to say that would improve this company, please tell us. We welcome you to tell us now."

"You hired me!" he'd begin, as if that was suitable explanation for what followed. "You should trust what I'm doing!"

"Trust and verify," Naveen would shoot back. "Trust *and verify.*"

In the end, it was the people working most closely with these executives who ultimately showed us that we couldn't keep them on. When Jason yelled at Jackie, our VP of HR, and when the top two business development reps quit, following one of Larry's outbursts, Naveen and I knew for certain that they needed to be let go.

Then there's Solomon—then VP of services and our prize hire from that period—who is still with us to this day, serving as our chief operating officer. The difference between Solomon and the others is dramatic. Not only does he do excellent work, but he's careful with the people around him. He's exactly the type of leader we most want to recruit and promote.

It's taken almost a decade for us to do what was necessary once we made the decision to drive the business forward. Even during the peak of the COVID-19 pandemic, we managed to keep building and growing our product and support, gaining more and more validation from the market. According to Gartner, a third-party reviewer, we graduated from the "visionary" quadrant to its "leader" quadrant, a shift that, as I understand it, means the world in our ability to scale our product and pursue additional growth. We're competing with billion-dollar companies—swimming with the sharks, as Naveen says. Today, there's an industry-recognized need for our product. Major companies are continuing to grow revenue and reduce operational costs by working with us.

Ultimately, we want Solumina to live and grow and for our company to make its customers and employees happy. I am so proud that Naveen is skilled at thinking through the long-term legacy of his father's company. And I can see, now, that he even demonstrated that skill in his personal life. Here is a guy who, at only twenty-five years old, moved into his current home with the thought that he was investing in a property right next to the schools his children would one day attend. Ever since he became an adult, he's been setting himself up not to have to worry.

CHAPTER 18

I often think about us finding the opportunity to make a well-timed exit from the company, allowing Naveen the freedom to do whatever he wants thereafter. Maybe start a new venture, go wherever his heart directs him. I can see that he has it in his blood to do a lot more with his life. But I see, too, that he wants balance, and I hope he finds it while he's still young.

The company that today is iBase-t was Amrik's dream, not Naveen's. Naveen and I have done right by that dream and seen it through to its success, but each of us may yet have other things we'd like to pursue. Still, to see that Amrik's vision continues to be compelling has become a part of who we are.

When we do eventually sell the company, I'll make that promised donation to UC Riverside in support of the endowed chair in Amrik's name. But I'll be sure not to let Mohit know anything about it.

After all this time, I've finally stopped thinking that every decision that's made about the company is a matter of life and death. More than twenty years ago, I had to be so very cautious. I didn't have any specialized knowledge to fall back on, and Naveen and I couldn't afford to lose whatever income I drew from the business. All I had was my determination to do what I thought Amrik would have done, along with the commonsense lessons I'd learned from my parents and my career experience as an obstetrics nurse. Of course, I still track the money going in and out, and I still like to keep an eye on our hiring processes and help address any employee issues that arise. As long as I'm part of the company, I will continue to do these things. That's just who I am.

Naveen has been growing his own family for almost a decade now. He has a wise and beautiful wife, and already I have two grandchildren to adore. I don't know how Naveen manages—running the company, traveling around the world, being present for his wife and their two girls, staying fit and sane. I had one child, and that was enough for me!

As one of nine myself, I'd witnessed how difficult it was for my parents to see to all our needs, and that's true even though my mother was able to hire help! Amrik and I tried for eight years before Naveen was conceived, and knowing from my job as a nurse and a midwife all that could go wrong with a pregnancy and delivery, I'd been easily convinced of my own likelihood of dying during childbirth. Having dealt primarily with high-risk pregnancies, I'd witnessed firsthand some worst-case scenarios. So Amrik and I didn't try for more children after Naveen, and we were both happy with that decision. Naveen has always been and will always be my priority, the son for whose sake I've directed all my actions both before and since Amrik's passing.

Back when Naveen was still in college, he found a street cat at school and brought it home to me. I didn't want it, but all too quickly that cat became my dear pet. Not long thereafter, I made the error in judgment that many cat owners make: I came to believe my cat would thrive if it had a companion. Those two cats had the best food, the best vet, the best filtered water to drink. They each lived to a ripe old age, even though

I understood from the start that Naveen had brought me that street cat so that I'd be preoccupied by it, and he could spend more time with his then girlfriend. Through the years—even as a young child—Naveen has been good at distracting me to his own advantage. I can still sense when he's coaxing me into a position or opinion that he'd like me to have. We might be just talking about which restaurant to take the family to for dinner, or maybe we're reviewing budgetary changes for the coming year; either way, I'm onto him.

It's in light of Naveen's ability to convince me even when I have my doubts that I'm still making the case that he should keep me engaged in all the major business decisions. But I see, too, that he'd be so very capable of independently leading the company if I were to withdraw entirely from it. Sometimes I think about how nice it would be to just drop by the office with some vegetables and flowers from the garden or with some of my Trinidadian soup—with veggies, chicken wings, potatoes, a salad, rolls, and dessert—and treat the group to lunch. I'd stop by the desks of our dearest employees for a bit of chitchat before heading out to lunch with Naveen, or to a tennis match with Janey, or back home for some time spent tending to the garden.

Just as I haven't yet given up on maintaining a role in the business, I also haven't given up my inclination to give people multiple opportunities to succeed. Perhaps the greatest bene-ficiary of this tendency of mine—more so than even Nick—is my gardener, Reuben. He's been with me for a quarter century, and for the majority of that time I've been running behind him, taking care of all the details he misses. A patch of grass will be dying, but he won't check to see that the sprinklers are functional unless I ask. I'll have placed new plants still in their pots exactly where I want them to be planted, but unless I tell him, "Reuben, please plant those new roses here and here," weeks will go by without him touching them. When he cuts the plants too short, I'll start watering them myself so that they don't get shocked. I don't mind following after him to do more gardening myself; it's my passion. I can see exactly what's needed and take care of it easily enough.

I've even offered Reuben's services to the neighbors; he takes care of about five homes on our street. Please don't mistake me: I like my neighbors—at the very least, to the extent that I don't want their lawns to die. And I do always remind them: "Make sure you're explicit with Reuben about what you need him to do."

When I wonder whether there's a "next step" for me, I can imagine owning a flower shop. Frankly, at first, I imagined owning a roti shop. A roti is like a burrito, an unleavened bread filled with ingredients like split peas, garbanzo beans, potatoes, maybe a protein like chicken or beef. I think a roti shop would be a great addition to our community. My childhood friend Angeline, who is still my close friend today—her mother made the best rotis. Angeline and I have even talked about going into business together. But the restaurant business is tough. You have to want to focus on it and nothing else.

Plus, not wanting exactly that is why I left Trinidad and went to England in the first place! Angeline and I would be marvelous at making rotis, but no. No, no, no.

There is another possibility I've considered, to which Naveen is the one who says, "No, no, no," and that's opening a nursing home. "You're not going to leave me with *that* responsibility!" he argues.

But a flower or garden shop? That's more difficult to put out of mind. I can easily picture my granddaughters having fun working there with me, then later on their own. Eventually, they could run it.

For now, when I'm not at work, I spend time keeping up with my friends and my Trinidadian family. I'm even helping to plan a reunion with some of my fellow nursing school friends. That trip will be the first time most of us have seen one another in fifty years. To this day, Janey and I visit weekly, mostly on Saturdays. We hit the tennis ball around or go for a walk around the lake, maybe stop for coffee and a muffin afterward. Sometimes she'll come over for breakfast and I'll pick us fruit from the garden—guavas, mandarins, oranges—and we'll enjoy the sunshine and some iced tea.

When it comes to family, I'm in closest touch with my eldest sister's firstborn, Yvonne, the niece with whom I grew up spending time during summers and holiday visits. Today, Yvonne is my steady link to Trinidad. We connect every other week, and she keeps me informed about all the other family members. My brother Elijah, the talented mechanic and now also an imam, and my eldest sister, Sarina, are both still alive. Sarina insists that no one but Yvonne be responsible for her care, and Yvonne obliges her. And though Elijah long ago arranged a permanent visa to come to the States, he never did. He's happy with his life in Trinidad, but I still think he could have been happy here in the US too. We lost Hana to ovarian cancer over a decade ago, but Zarine passed just two years back; she fell, hit her head, and died of a brain hemorrhage, just like our father. Russell passed a few years ago too. He had colon cancer but didn't have faith in his doctor and refused to follow up on his care options.

As I look back on my life, I can see that during circumstances I wish would have been otherwise, I discovered a strength I did not know I had. And I learned that my strength grew directly from the desire to do the best I could to carry on, to carry forward Amrik's plans and establish his legacy, to see that Naveen wouldn't hurt for resources and opportunities, and, most of all, to earn my son's respect.

I didn't take the obvious way out. I didn't immediately sell the company, get the money, and find something easier to do. I'm proud to have turned over to my son a profitable company with no debt. I am proud that I didn't just try; I worked hard at it. Failure was never an option when it came to providing for my family and keeping my true love's dreams alive.

Add to that the fact that I've been lucky enough to witness my son's success, and perhaps you'll understand why I hope that my story will inspire my grandchildren, and maybe even generations yet to come.

EPILOGUE

Naveen tells me that one of the things he's been most surprised to discover while running his father's business is that you really can "fake it till you make it." By that, I think he means that you don't know what you don't know, but common sense, determination, and desire can help keep you afloat as you figure out what you need to learn. I started out not knowing how to turn on a computer, then led a software company for decades.

Of all that I've learned along the way, I've been most surprised by the connections between taking care of people's pains as their nurse and taking care of people's pains in a business setting. In both instances, one needs to find ways not only to alleviate those pains but also to motivate those suffering from them to believe that things will get better. Careful listening is at the heart of both activities, as is ensuring that you take meaningful action in response to what you discover.

I've learned, too, that so much happens that simply cannot be anticipated. At my best, I tried to figure out one problem at a time, ideally with the aid of other problem solvers rather than being left to my own devices. I've relied on the help and care of so many people, from Frederick to Vanessa, my lawyer and Jai, and the group of loyal employees who always made sure I knew what I needed to know.

Along the way, we had to take our licks and make good on what other companies have shown us still needs work. I learned that staying focused on the goal helps determine the steps for getting there and keeps the motivation alive.

There have been life lessons alongside those business lessons. I offer them here just as when I chased Naveen around the house or the office, trying to confirm that he heard me:

Don't let obstacles get in the way of what you desire. Roads can be rocky, pathways unmarked, but you'll find that you are strong enough to face whatever challenges come your way to get wherever you want to in life. And should your desire meet opportunity? Go for it!

Often, you can't know what you have in you until you test your ability. You may find that your limitations and your strengths are different from what you thought they were or expected them to be.

Learn something about your roots. My mother was not formally educated, but she was the consummate businessperson. What instincts and skills I had in this area, I believe I drew from her.

If you're willing to work, you will make it in life. Just don't expect a short or easy journey.

Ignore petty naysayers. They're either secretly jealous or outright rooting for you to fail just so they can think of themselves as superior to you.

Don't hang yourself with any of the opportunities you're given. I ran through the pros and cons of every difficult decision I had to make with the question in mind: Will I hang myself if I do this? *Doing so offered me a path to clarity in situations where otherwise I struggled to find my way.*

It can feel like the end of the world when you're grieving or going through difficult times. Sometimes the resources for coping turn up in unanticipated places: The persistent kindness of friends. The reassurance from a former employer that even if you got turned out onto the street, they would help you find work.

Focus on what you suspect, or know, really matters. What kept me motivated was the survival of the company and the overall well-being of the people working there. I didn't worry about matters of ego or amassing a fortune.

Take calculated risks, no matter what you're doing. I didn't know I would become CEO of a tech company. But I got up to speed, stuck with it, and learned from people around me.

By now, maybe you know the one bit of advice on which I'll end. My mother offered it to me, I've repeated it to Naveen, and now I give it to you:

Always, always save for a rainy day.

ACKNOWLEDGMENTS

To my late husband, Amrik, whose memory continues to guide me every day: This memoir is as much yours as it is mine. You taught me how to lead, love, persevere, and trust myself over anyone else. You remain in my heart, and this book is a tribute to you.

To my father, for being my guiding light and always wanting better for me. I always have your voice in my head before making any major decisions. And though you are no longer in our presence, everything I do, I do to make you proud.

To my mother, for instilling in me the strength of character that has seen me through my toughest times, and for teaching me to work hard and depend only on myself.

To my sisters, for their love and support through our childhood and adulthood, in good times and bad. You are in my heart forever.

To the Mann family, you are my guardian angels and more than family to me. With your unconditional love and support, no matter the time of day or night, you have been by my side through the toughest times, caring for me, reassuring me, and never letting me feel alone. I am forever grateful to you all.

To my friends both near and far, you have offered me a safe

space to heal and remind me that I am not alone in this journey. I am forever grateful for your compassion and understanding.

To the incredible team at iBase-t that I've had the privilege of working with throughout my career, thank you for your belief in me. The legacy of my late husband and the work we built together would not have been possible without your contributions, and I carried it forward with utmost pride and responsibility. Confident and ready to pass on the baton to Naveen.

To Naveen and Insiyah, my son and daughter-in-law. Thank you for your encouragement and unwavering support, not only in pushing me to publish my story, but in all other aspects of our lives together. Naveen, you are my rock, my diamond, and you constantly exceed my expectations. I know your father is watching over us and beaming with pride at your many accomplishments.

My wonderful granddaughters, Aaliya and Samara, you have brought so much light, laughter, and joy into my life. May this book inspire, uplift, and help you navigate your own journeys with love and resilience.

Jennifer Holt, thank you for helping me bring my story to life. I couldn't have done this without you.

A special thanks to the readers who will pick up this book, for allowing me the honor of sharing my story.

With all my love and gratitude,

Ladeira

ABOUT THE AUTHOR

LADEIRA POONIAN started her career as a registered nurse and earned an RNC degree to work with patients with high-risk pregnancies. After twenty-eight years of nursing experience, she stepped into the role of CEO and chairman of the board after her husband tragically passed away in 1998. The Overnight CEO is the story of her journey.